Knitting
OUTSIDE THE
Swatch

40
MODERN MOTIFS

Kristin Omdahl

INTERWEAVE
interweave.com

EDITOR Michelle Bredeson

TECHNICAL EDITOR Kay Mariea

ASSOCIATE ART DIRECTOR Julia Boyles

COVER AND INTERIOR DESIGN
Lora Lamm & Kristin Lipman

BEAUTY PHOTOGRAPHER Joe Hancock

SWATCH PHOTOGRAPHER Joe Coca

PHOTO STYLIST Emily Smoot

HAIR AND MAKEUP Kathy MacKay

ILLUSTRATOR Timm Bryson

PRODUCTION Katherine Jackson

Interweave
A division of F+W Media, Inc.
201 East Fourth Street
Loveland, CO 80537
interweave.com

Manufactured in China by RR Donnelley Shenzhen.

Library of Congress Cataloging-in-Publication Data

Omdahl, Kristin.
   Knitting outside the swatch : 40 modern motifs /
Kristin Omdahl.
      pages cm
   Includes index.
   ISBN 978-1-59668-793-6 (pbk.)
   ISBN 978-1-59668-890-2 (PDF)
   1. Knitting--Patterns. I. Title.
   TT825.O4385 2013
   746.43'2--dc23
                              2013010972

10 9 8 7 6 5 4 3 2 1

TO MARLON, MY SHARK HUNTER.
As you become a young man instead of my baby boy, you continue to inspire me and challenge me to be the best person I can be. I only hope I make you proud, too. I love you with all my heart and soul.

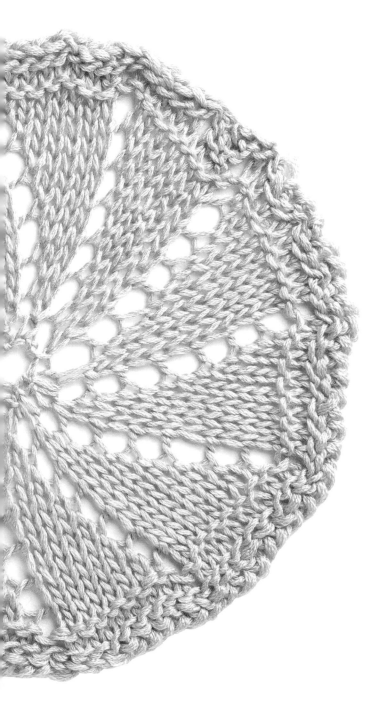

ACKNOWLEDGMENTS

Thank you to the incredibly talented team at Interweave. You take my stitches, words, and fabrics and turn them into books I am so proud to share with the world. A special thank-you to Allison Korleski for believing in me and this book. I appreciate that through all the changes outside of our control this year, you never left my side. Thank you to Michelle Bredeson for being patient with my travel schedule this year and for being so supportive of this book.

Thank you to Jennifer Edgar of Eucalan for giving me the wonderful opportunity to design and develop Wrapture this year. I believe so strongly in this product and the benefits of an eco-friendly delicate wash for properly caring for the luxury fibers we work so hard to knit. I'm proud to say I am friends with each of the yarn companies who generously donated their beautiful yarns for the motifs and projects in this collection. Thanks to Lantern Moon for donating the gorgeous rosewood double-pointed and circular knitting needles I used to create the pieces in this book.

Lynnea Argyle-Lace Pullover

CONTENTS

Thora Lace Cardigan

Zuna Starburst Shrug

Introduction

This book is an exploration of techniques for creating flowers, circles, squares, and other shapes and combining them to form visually stunning two-dimensional fabrics and three-dimensional garments.

I love knitting motif swatches. They're small and quick to make, allowing you to experiment with new stitch patterns and techniques without a big commitment in time and yarn. Best of all, they're so versatile. Create a beautiful embellishment to a sweater with a single flower motif; seam together an assortment of squares to create an afghan; transform a circular motif into the crown of a hat; trim a shawl with a lacy motif for a striking edging. The possibilities are endless.

The motifs I've designed are different sizes and shapes, involve a variety of construction approaches, and support a range of stitching styles. Some are worked in the round from the center out, some in the round from the perimeter in, and some in rows. The motifs are organized by shape, with chapters on flower and star motifs; circles, squares, and rectangles; assorted unusual shapes; and motifs that join as you go to create seamless fabric. Within those shapes, I've explored various stitch patterns, including cables, lace, short-rows, and more.

Inspired by the geometry of some of the forty motifs, I created a ten-project collection of garments and accessories. There are far more motifs than projects, so feel free to mix and match them to create your own original designs. For some of the projects, I've included tips to help you make substitutions.

This book is only the beginning. You can follow the patterns, interchange the motifs used in the patterns with slight modifications, or explore and create your own fabric and garments for complete creative control. Grab your needles and start **Knitting Outside the Swatch!**

Tindra Herringbone Scarf

How to Use the Motifs

I'VE TAKEN TEN OF MY FAVORITE motifs and used them as the basis for the projects in this book, but there are so many more possibilities. Here are some ways to approach designing with motifs.

Allover Fabric

The most obvious way to use the motifs is to join a large number of them together to create fabric. Squares and rectangles butted together will form a solid fabric, reminiscent of a patchwork quilt. Circles, flowers, and other irregularly shaped motifs will form open airy fabric. If you prefer a more dense look, you can fill in the open areas with smaller motifs. Use the fabric to make pillows, afghans, baby blankets, shawls, and elements of garments. Several projects in this book are created this way, included the Fiola Flower Shawl (page 108) and the Tindra Herringbone Scarf (page 114).

Edgings

Many of the motifs in this collection would make beautiful edgings. I've used a number of the motifs as edgings in projects, including the Siri Möbius Cowl (page 78) and the Kiara Tile-Edged Shawl (page 94). The motifs can be sewn on after the main piece is complete, knit as an extension of the garment, or even knit first then joined to create the edging. If you plan to substitute motifs, make sure they have the same number of stitches and/or sides or make adjustments to compensate, such as using more or fewer motifs.

Embellishments

On their own or grouped together, motifs make wonderful embellishments to handknits or even purchased garments. Many of the motifs in the Flowers & Stars section (page 12) are ideal for using as embellishments. A single flower motif would transform a simple beanie into a chic accessory. Several flower motifs clustered together could liven up an otherwise plain sweater. Dress them up even more by adding beautiful beads or buttons as centers.

Focal Points

A striking motif creates a dramatic focal point for a project. For the Zuna Starburst Shrug (page 82), I joined together four large motifs and designed a shrug around them, but one large square motif would have worked just as well. Try using a circular or hexagonal motif as the crown of a hat or as an inset in a sweater. Join two large motifs together to create an accent pillow or a cute purse. Enlarge a single circle into an unusual afghan. This is a great opportunity to think outside the swatch.

Zuna Starburst Shrug

you find the perfect arrangement. A crocheted join can also make a nice accent if you use a different color yarn. For the Zuna Starburst Shrug (page 82), I knit four Square Starburst motifs (page 39) separately, sewed them together, then picked up stitches all around the motifs to knit the shrug.

Joining Live Stitches
If you leave the stitches on the needles, or "live," you can join them using Kitchener stitch or three-needle bind-off. Either of these methods creates a virtually invisible join.

Picking Up and Knitting
This is one of my favorite joining methods because it creates a cleaner join than seaming but requires less planning ahead than joining live stitches. I used this method for several projects, including the Tindra Herringbone Scarf (page 114). Try to pick up evenly across a length of fabric for a neat look.

JOINING METHODS
Just as there are many different ways to work with motifs, there are a number of methods for joining them together. See the Glossary (page 129) for illustrations of these joining methods.

Seaming
The most basic way to join motifs is to knit them separately, then sew or crochet them together. The advantages of this method are that you can work on a number of motifs over time and put them together when you're ready. If you're combining motifs knit in different colors or with different stitch patterns, joining them all together at the end allows you to rearrange them until

Joining as You Go
For my seamless motifs (page 54), I pick up and knit into the last motif, then knit the new stitch together with the adjacent stitch, so I'm not actually increasing but creating a solid join. You can create an endless row of motifs in this way and even combine them into multiple rows. I used this method for the Lynnea Argyle-Lace Pullover (page 102) and the Thora Lace Cardigan (page 120).

TIP
I knit all of the motifs on size U.S. 8 (5 mm) needles with Naturally Caron Country, a worsted-weight merino/acrylic blend yarn, or Caron Simply Soft, a worsted-weight acrylic yarn (the Join-as-You-Go motifs, page 54). Try knitting them in yarns with different weights and fiber contents and mix up the needle sizes to create completely different effects.

Siri Möbius Cowl

Flowers & Stars

Living in Florida, I spend a lot of time outdoors. I'm constantly inspired by the beauty of nature and often incorporate natural shapes into my designs. Flowers and stars are fun motifs to knit because they can stand on their own or be joined together to create gorgeous lacy fabrics.

SWAGGED FLOWER

CO 14 sts.

Row 1: (K2, p2) 3 times, k2.

Row 2: (P2, k2) 3 times, p2.

NOTE: *Work short-rows in sets of 2 rows until 4 sts remain as follows:*

Row 3: (K2, p2) 3 times, turn (do not complete row).

Row 4: (K2, p2) 3 times.

Row 5: (K2, p2) 2 times, k2, turn (do not complete row).

Row 6: (P2, k2) 2 times, p2.

Row 7: (K2, p2) 2 times, turn (do not complete row).

Row 8: (K2, p2) 2 times.

Row 9: K2, p2, k2, turn (do not complete row).

Row 10: P2, k2, p2.

Row 11: K2, p2, turn (do not complete row).

Row 12: K2, p2.

Row 13: Rep Row 1.

Wrap yarn around sts 3 times before continuing (see Glossary).

Row 14: Rep Row 2.

Rep Rows 3–14 four more times.

Rep Rows 3–13 once more.

BO all sts in pattern, leaving long tail (about 12" [30.5 cm]).

Sew CO and BO edges together to form a ring. Wrap yarn around sts over the seam 3 times (like the other wraps), ending at the center. Insert needle under and through all 6 wraps and cinch to bring the center together. Fasten off securely.

GARDENIA FLOWER

Flower Center

Row 1: Make a slipknot, knit into the front, back, front, back, front, back—6 sts.

Rows 2, 4, 6: Knit.

Row 3: K1f&b 6 times—12 sts.

Row 5: K1f&b 12 times—24 sts.

Petals

Set-up row: CO 5 sts using knitted CO (see Glossary).

Row 1: K4, k2tog with live st on Row 6 of flower center.

Row 2: Turn, k4, yo, k1f&b—7 petal sts.

Row 3: K6, k2tog with next live st on Row 6 of flower center.

Row 4: Turn, k6, yo, k1f&b—9 petal sts.

Row 5: K8, k2tog with next live st on Row 6 of flower center.

Row 6: Turn, k8, yo, k1f&b—11 petal sts.

Row 7: K10, k2tog with next live st on Row 6 of flower center.

Row 8: Turn, k10, yo, k1f&b—13 petal sts.

Row 9: BO 8 sts, k4, k2tog with next live st on Row 6 of flower center.

Rep rows 2–9 five more times.

With another needle, pick up 5 sts along the original petal CO row. Then holding original CO edge and last row together, BO using three-needle BO technique (see Glossary), leaving long tail for sewing the 6 rows of the flower center.

SIX-PETAL LACE FLOWER

First Petal

Row 1: Make a slipknot, knit into the front, back, and front of loop—3 sts.

Rows 2 4, 6, 8, 10: (WS) Purl.

Row 3: (RS) K1, yo, k1, yo, k1—5 sts.

Row 5: K2, yo, k1, yo, k2—7 sts.

Row 7: K3, yo, k1, yo, k3—9 sts.

Row 9: K4, yo, k1, yo, k4—11 sts.

Row 11: K1, ssk, knit across to last 3 sts, k2tog, k1—9 sts.

Row 12: P1, p2tog, purl across to last 3 sts; p2tog, p1—7 sts.

Row 13: K1, ssk, knit across to last 3 sts, k2tog, k1—5 sts.

Cut yarn and place partial petal on stitch holder or extra needle.

Second through Fifth Petals

Repeat first petal.

Sixth Petal

Rep first petal, but do not cut yarn. Place the 5 sts for each of the 6 petals on same needle—30 sts.

Next row: (WS) Purl across—30 sts.

Next row: (RS) K2tog across—15 sts.

Next row: P2tog across to last 3 sts; p3tog—7 sts.

Next row: K2tog 2 times, k3tog—3 sts.

Next row: K3tog, fasten off, leaving long tail. Sew seam along the last 4 sts between the first and sixth petals.

EIGHT-POINT EYELET STAR

CO 9 sts.

Row 1: Ssk, k6, k1f&b—9 sts.

Row 2: K1, (yo, k2tog) 4 times—9 sts.

Rows 3–9: Rep Rows 1–2 three more times, then rep Row 1 once more.

BO 9 sts. Do not fasten off last st on needle.

＊Keeping last st on needle, turn work 90 degrees counter clockwise and evenly pick up 8 sts along the side edge—9 sts.

Rows 1–9: Rep Rows 1–9 of previous parallelogram. BO 9 sts. Do not fasten off last st.

Rep from ＊ 6 more times. Cut yarn, leaving long tail. Sew seam.

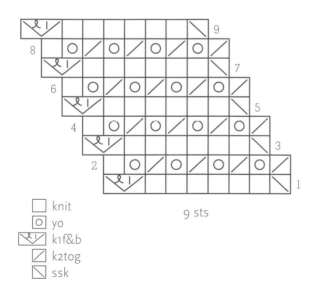

9 sts

	knit
O	yo
	k1f&b
/	k2tog
\	ssk

TIP
Try overlapping multiple flowers and tacking them down to create a pretty textured edging along a hem or neckline.

(as featured in Fiola Flower Shawl at right and on page 108)

SHORT-ROW FLOWER

First Petal

CO 13 sts using knitted CO (see Glossary).

Row 1: K13.

Row 2: K7, turn, k2, turn, k3, turn, k4, turn, k5, turn, k6, turn, k7, turn, k8, turn, k9, turn, k10, turn, k11, turn, k12, turn, k13.

Second Petal

*CO 13 sts using knitted CO.

Row 1: K13.

Row 2: K7, turn, k2, turn, k3, turn, k4, turn, k5, turn, k6, turn, k7, turn, k8, turn, k9, turn, k10, turn, k11, turn, k12, turn, k13.

Rep from * 6 more times, for a total of 8 petals—104 sts.

Next row: K2tog across—52 sts.

Next row: K2tog across—26 sts.

Next row: *Yo 3 times, k2tog. Rep from * across—26 sts.

Next row: Drop extra loops for each yo st, k2tog across —13 sts.

*Pass second to last st up and over last st. Rep from * until only 1 st remains on needle. Fasten off. Sew 2 rows of petal 1 to 2 rows of petal 8 to form circle.

SIX-PETAL PINWHEEL FLOWER

CO 3 sts.

Row 1: (RS) K1f&b, k2—4 sts.

Row 2 (and all even-numbered rows): (WS) Purl.

Row 3: K1f&b, k3—5 sts.

Row 5: K1f&b, k4—6 sts.

Row 7: K1f&b, k5—7 sts.

Row 9: BO 4 sts, k3—3 sts.

Rows 11–58: Rep Rows 1–10 four more times, then 1–8 once more—6 sharp petal ends.

Row 59: BO all sts; do not fasten off.

Flower Center

Row 1: Turn 90 degrees and working in the straight side of rows, pick up and knit (see Glossary) 30 sts evenly across (about 1 st every 2 rows)—30 sts.

Row 2: P2tog across—15 sts.

Row 3: *Lift second st over first st and off needle. Rep from * across. Fasten off last st. Sew original 3 CO sts to last 3 BO sts to join.

> ### TIP
> One of my ideas for creating the three different sizes of the Pinwheel Flower motif was to stack them together and secure them to create a three-dimensional flower. You could also use a single flower as an embellishment or cluster multiple motifs for an organic look.

EIGHT-PETAL PINWHEEL FLOWER

CO 5 sts.

Row 1: (RS) K1f&b, k4—6 sts.

Row 2 (and all even-numbered rows): (WS) Purl.

Row 3: K1f&b, k5—7 sts.

Row 5: K1f&b, k6—8 sts.

Row 7: K1f&b, k7—9 sts.

Row 9: BO 4 sts, k5—5 sts.

Rows 11–88: Rep Rows 1–10 seven more times, Rows 1–8 once more—8 sharp petal ends.

Row 89: BO all sts; do not fasten off.

Flower Center

Row 1: Turn 90 degrees and working in the straight side of rows, pick up and knit (see Glossary) 45 sts evenly across (about 1 st every 2 rows)—45 sts.

Row 2: P3tog across row—15 sts.

Row 3: *Lift second st over first st and off needle. Rep from * across. Fasten off last st. Sew flower center seam and the original 3 CO sts to last 3 BO sts.

TWELVE-PETAL PINWHEEL FLOWER

CO 7 sts.

Row 1: (RS) K1f&b, k6—8 sts.

Row 2 (and all even-numbered rows): (WS) Purl.

Row 3: K1f&b, k7—9 sts.

Row 5: K1f&b, k8—10 sts.

Row 7: K1f&b, k9—11 sts.

Row 9: BO 4 sts, k7—7 sts.

Rows 11–118: Rep Rows 1–10 ten more times, Rows 1–8 once more—12 sharp petal ends.

Row 119: BO all sts; do not fasten off.

Flower Center

Row 1: Turn 90 degrees and working in the straight side of rows, pick up and knit (see Glossary) 60 sts evenly across (about 1 st every 2 rows)—60 sts.

Row 2: P2tog across row—30 sts.

Row 3: K2tog across row—15 sts.

Row 4: ✱Lift second st over first st and off needle. Rep from ✱ across. Fasten off last st. Sew flower center seam and the 7 CO sts to last 7 BO sts.

EIGHT-POINT GARTER-STITCH STAR

First Parallelogram

CO 9 sts.

Row 1: Ssk, k6, k1f&b—9 sts.

Row 2: Knit.

Rows 3–9: Rep Rows 1–2 three more times, then rep Row 1 once more.

*CO 3 sts using knitted CO (see Glossary), BO 3 sts, place st back on left needle. Rep from * 2 more times. BO all rem sts. Do not fasten off last st on needle.

Second Parallelogram

**Keeping last st on needle, turn work 90 degrees counter-clockwise and evenly pick up 8 sts along side edge—9 sts.

Rows 1–9: Rep Rows 1–9 of previous parallelogram. *CO 3 sts using knitted CO, BO 3 sts, place st back on left needle. Rep from * 2 more times. BO all rem sts. Do not fasten off last st on needle.

Rep from ** 6 more times. Cut yarn, leaving long tail. Sew seam.

> **TIP**
> Make multiple motifs and join them at the tips as you knit to create a lacy fabric perfect for a scarf, shawl, or throw.

ROUND FLOWER MEDALLION

Using dpn, make slipknot, knit into front and back of loop until you have 12 sts. Divide sts over 3 or 4 dpn, join without twisting, and pm for beg of rnd.

Rnd 1: Knit.

Rnd 2: *Yo, k1. Rep from * around—24 sts.

Rnd 3 (and all odd-numbered rnds): Knit.

Rnd 4: *K2, (k1, yo, k1) in same st, k1. Rep from * around—36 sts.

Rnd 6: *K3, (k1, yo, k1) in same st, k2. Rep from * around—48 sts.

Rnd 8: *K4, (k1, yo, k1) in same st, k3. Rep from * around—60 sts.

Rnd 10: *Yo, ssk, k6, k2tog. Rep from * around.

Rnd 11: *Knit into front and back of yo, k8. Rep from * around—60 sts.

TIP

Seam together multiple motifs to create a gorgeous afghan. Try knitting the motifs in a variety of colors for a dazzling effect.

Rnd 12: *(Yo, k1) 2 times, yo, ssk, k4, k2tog. Rep from * around—66 sts.

Rnd 14: *(Yo, k1) 5 times, yo, ssk, k2, k2tog. Rep from * around—90 sts.

Rnd 16: *(Yo, k2tog) 5 times, yo, k1, yo, s2k2p. Rep from * around—84 sts.

Rnd 17: Knit.

Rnd 18: Purl.

BO loosely in knit.

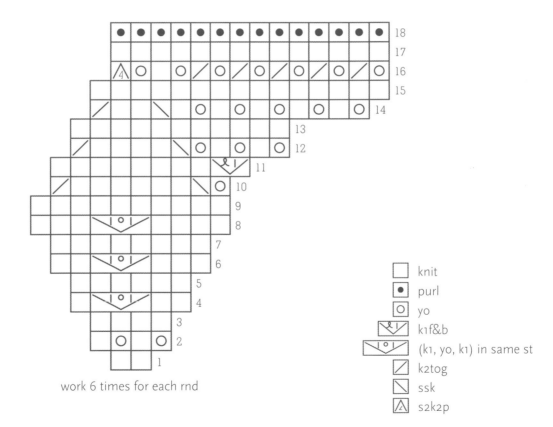

work 6 times for each rnd

	knit
•	purl
o	yo
	k1f&b
	(k1, yo, k1) in same st
/	k2tog
\	ssk
/\	s2k2p

HEXAGON FLOWER MEDALLION

With dpns, make a slipknot and place on knitting needle. With a second needle, work (k1, p1) 6 times into slipknot. Divide sts over 3 dpn, join without twisting, and pm for beg of rnd.

Rnd 1: Knit—12 sts.

Rnd 2: (Yo, k1) around—24 sts.

Rnd 3 (and all odd-numbered rnds): Knit.

Rnd 4: *K2, (k1, yo, k1) into same st, k1. Repeat from * 6 times—36 sts.

Rnd 6: *K3, (k1, yo, k1) into same st, k2. Repeat from * 6 times—48 sts.

Rnd 8: *K4, (k1, yo, k1) into same st, k3. Repeat from * 6 times—60 sts.

Rnd 10: *K5, (k1, yo, k1) into same st, k4. Repeat from * 6 times—72 sts.

Rnd 12: *K6, (k1, yo, k1) into same st, k5. Repeat from * 6 times—84 sts.

Rnd 14: *K7, (k1, yo, k1) into same st, k6. Repeat from * 6 times—96 sts.

Rnd 16: *K1, yo, ssk, k11, k2tog, yo. Repeat from * 6 times—96 sts.

NOTE: *Switch to circular needles at this point, or when you feel comfortable.*

Rnd 18: *(K1, yo) 2 times, ssk, k9, k2tog, yo, k1, yo. Repeat from * 6 times—108 sts.

Rnd 20: *K1, yo, k2tog, yo, k1, yo, ssk, k7, (k2tog, yo) 2 times, k1, yo. Repeat from * 6 times—120 sts.

Rnd 22: *K1, (yo, k2tog) 2 times, yo, k1, yo, ssk, k5, (k2tog, yo) 3 times, k1, yo. Repeat from * 6 times—132 sts.

Rnd 24: *K1, (yo, k2tog) 3 times, yo, k1, yo, ssk, k3, (k2tog, yo) 4 times, k1, yo. Repeat from * 6 times—144 sts.

Rnd 26: *K1, (yo, k2tog) 4 times, yo, k1, yo, ssk, k1, (k2tog, yo) 5 times, k1, yo. Repeat from * 6 times—156 sts.

Rnd 28: *K1, (yo, k2tog) 5 times, yo, k1, yo, s2kp, (yo, k2tog) 5 times, yo, k1, yo. Repeat from * 6 times—168 sts.

Rnd 30: *K1, (yo, k2tog) 13 times, yo, k1, yo—180 sts.

Rnd 32: *K1, yo, k29, yo. Repeat from * 6 times—192 sts.

BO: K1, *yo, k1. Slip the yo and the first st over the last st and off needle. Repeat from * around. Cut yarn and pull through last st to fasten off.

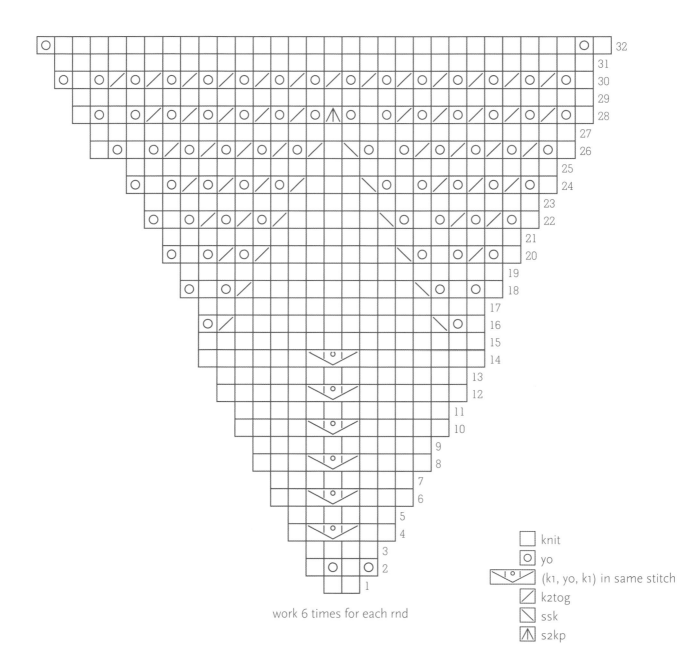

work 6 times for each rnd

	knit
O	yo
	(k1, yo, k1) in same stitch
/	k2tog
\	ssk
∧	s2kp

Circles, Squares & Rectangles

These basic shapes are probably the simplest motifs to create. They make wonderful canvases for a multitude of techniques and stitch patterns and great foundations for a variety of projects.

SMALL RIBBED CIRCLE

Using dpn, make a slipknot. (k1, p1) 4 times in slipknot—8 sts. Divide sts over 4 dpn, join without twisting, and pm for beg of rnd.

Rnd 1: *K1, p1. Rep from * around.

Rnd 2: *K1f&b, pfb. Rep from * around—16 sts.

Rnd 3: *K2, p2. Rep from * around—16 sts.

Rnd 4: *(K1f&b, p1) in same st, (p1, k1f&b) in same st, p2. Rep from * around—32 sts.

Rnds 5–7: *K2, p2. Rep from * around.

Rnd 8: *K2, (pfb, k1) in same st, (k1, pfb) in same st, k2, p2. Rep from * around—48 sts.

Rnds 9–11: *K2, p2. Rep from * around.

Rnd 12: *K2, p2, (k1f&b, p1) in same st, (p1, k1f&b) in same st, p2, k2, p2. Rep from * around—64 sts.

Rnds 13–15: *K2, p2. Rep from * around.

Rnd 16: *K2, p2, k2, (pfb, k1) in same st, (k1, pfb) in same st, (k2, p2) 2 times. Rep from * around—80 sts.

Rnds 17–20: *K2, p2. Rep from * around.

BO loosely in ribbing.

TIP
To create an unusual round afghan from a single motif, continue on with the established increases until you have the size circle you need. If a simple circle is too plain, dress it up by adding an edging around the entire perimeter.

LARGE RIBBED CIRCLE

Using dpn, make a slipknot. (K1, p1) 6 times in slipknot—12 sts. Divide sts over 4 dpn, join without twisting, and pm for beg of rnd.

Rnd 1: *K1, p1. Rep from * around.

Rnd 2: *K1f&b, pfb. Rep from * around—24 sts.

Rnd 3: *K2, p2. Rep from * around—24 sts.

Rnd 4: *(K1f&b, p1) in same st, (p1, k1f&b) in same st, p2. Rep from * around—48 sts.

Rnds 5–7: *K2, p2. Rep from * around.

Rnd 8: *K2, (pfb, k1) in same st, (k1, pfb) in same st, k2, p2. Rep from * around—72 sts.

Rnds 9–11: *K2, p2. Rep from * around.

Rnd 12: *K2, p2, (k1f&b, p1) in same st, (p1, k1f&b) in same st, p2, k2, p2. Rep from * around—96 sts.

Rnds 13–15: *K2, p2. Rep from * around.

Rnd 16: *K2, p2, k2, (pfb, k1) in same st, (k1, pfb) in same st, (k2, p2) 2 times. Rep from * around—120 sts.

Rnds 17–20: *K2, p2. Rep from * around.

BO loosely in ribbing.

SQUARE WITH I-CORD CENTER RING

Row 1: Using dpn, make a slipknot, knit into front, back, front, and back of loop—4 sts.

Row 2: Slip sts to other end of needle, k4.

Rows 3–40: Rep Row 2 for I-cord (see Glossary).

Fasten off, leaving long tail. Sew CO edge to BO edge to make a seamless ring.

Rnd 1: Pick up and knit into any edge st around tube, (yo, skip next row, pick up and knit into st in next row)—40 sts.

Rnd 2: *K9, yo, k1, yo. Rep from * 3 more times—48 sts.

Rnd 3: Knit.

Rnd 4: *K10, (yo, k1, yo, k11) 3 times, yo, k1, yo, k1—56 sts.

Rnd 5: Knit.

Rnd 6: *K11, (yo, k1, yo, k13) 3 times, yo, k1, yo, k2—64 sts.

Rnd 7: Knit.

Rnd 8: *K12, (yo, k1, yo, k15) 3 times, yo, k1, yo, k3—72 sts.

Rnd 9: Knit.

Rnd 10: *K13, (yo, k1, yo, k17) 3 times, yo, k1, yo, k4—80 sts.

Rnd 11: Purl.

BO loosely in knit. Fasten off.

TIP
Try playing around with color. The I-cord center ring would really pop graphically if knit in a different hue.

SQUARE WITH LACE-WHEEL CENTER

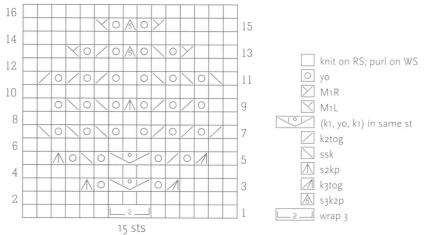

15 sts

knit on RS; purl on WS
yo
M1R
M1L
(k1, yo, k1) in same st
k2tog
ssk
s2kp
k3tog
s3k2p
wrap 3

CO 15 sts.

Row 1: (RS) K6, wrap 3, k6.

Row 2 (and all even-numbered rows): (WS) Purl.

Row 3: K4, k3tog, yo, (k1, yo, k1) in same st, yo, s2kp, k4.

Row 5: K2, k3tog, yo, k2tog, yo, (k1, yo, k1) in same st, yo, ssk, yo, s2kp, k2.

Row 7: K1, (k2tog, yo) 3 times, k1, (yo, ssk) 3 times, k1.

Row 9: K2, (yo, k2tog) 2 times, yo, s2kp, (yo, ssk) 2 times, yo, k2.

Row 11: K1, (ssk, yo) 3 times, k1, (yo, k2tog) 3 times, k1.

Row 13: K3, M1R, yo, ssk, yo, s3k2p, yo, k2tog, yo, M1L, k3.

Row 14: Purl.

Row 15: K5, M1R, yo, s3k2p, yo, M1L, k5.

Rnd 1: Using dpn, K15, turn, using second dpn, pick up and knit 16 sts along end of rows, turn, using third dpn, pick up and knit 15 sts in CO edge, turn, using fourth dpn, pick up and knit 16 sts along end of rows—62 sts.

Rnd 2: K1, yo, k13, yo, k3, yo, k12, yo, k3, yo, k13, yo, k3, yo, k12, yo, k2—70 sts.

Rnd 3: Knit.

Rnd 4: K1, yo, k15, yo, k3, yo, k14, yo, k3, yo, k15, yo, k3, yo, k14, yo, k2—78 sts.

Rnd 5: Knit.

Rnd 6: K1, yo, k17, yo, k3, yo, k16, yo, k3, yo, k17, yo, k3, yo, k16, yo, k2—86 sts.

Rnd 7: Knit.

Rnd 8: K1, yo, k19, yo, k3, yo, k18, yo, k3, yo, k19, yo, k3, yo, k18, yo, k2—94 sts.

Rnd 9: Knit.

Rnd 10: K1, yo, k21, yo, k3, yo, k20, yo, k3, yo, k21, yo, k3, yo, k20, yo, k2—102 sts.

Rnd 11: Purl.

BO loosely in knit. Fasten off.

(as featured in Selena Crescent Moon Shawlette at right and on page 90)

CRESCENT MOON

CO 7 sts.

Row 1: (RS) K1f&b in each st across—14 sts.

Row 2: (WS) K1f&b in each st across—28 sts.

Row 3: Knit.

Row 4: Purl.

Rows 5–12: Rep Rows 3–4.

BO as follows: *CO 3 sts using knitted CO (see Glossary), BO 6 sts. Rep from * across, CO 3 sts using knitted CO, BO 3 sts. Fasten off.

TIP
Make two half-circles and join them together to create a circle with an open center and double your design possibilities. Try joining multiple circles as you go to make a chain-link scarf.

RECTANGLE WITH GARTER-STITCH CENTER

Using dpn, CO 6 sts.

Row 1: Knit.

Rows 2–14: Rep Row 1.

Rnd 1: K6, turn, using second dpn, pick up and knit 14 sts along side edge of rows, turn, using third dpn, pick up and knit 6 sts along CO edge, turn, using fourth dpn, pick up and knit 14 sts along side edge of rows, turn. Join in round—40 sts.

Rnd 2: Knit.

Rnd 3: K6, yo, k1, yo, k12, yo, k1, yo, k6, yo, k1, yo, k12, yo, k1, yo—48 sts.

Rnd 4: Knit.

Rnd 5: K7, yo, k1, yo, k14, yo, k1, yo, k8, yo, k1, yo, k14, yo, k1, yo, k1—56 sts.

Rnd 6: Knit.

Rnd 7: K8, yo, k1, yo, k16, yo, k1, yo, k10, yo, k1, yo, k16, yo, k1, yo, k2—64 sts.

Rnd 8: Purl.

BO loosely in knit. Fasten off.

RECTANGLE WITH I-CORD CENTER

Row 1: Using dpn, make a slipknot and knit into front, back, front, and back of loop—4 sts.

Row 2: Slip sts to other end of needle, k4.

Rows 3–32: Rep Row 2 for I-cord (see Glossary).

Rnd 1: K4, turn, using second dpn, pick up and knit 16 sts along side of I-cord, turn, using third dpn, pick up and knit 4 sts along CO edge, turn, using fourth dpn, pick up and knit along side of I-cord, turn, join in round—40 sts.

Rnd 2: K4, kfbf, k14, kfbf, k4, kfbf, k14, kfbf—48 sts.

Rnd 3 (and all odd-numbered rnds): Purl.

Rnd 4: K5, kfbf, k16, kfbf, k6, kfbf, k16, kfbf, k1—56 sts.

Rnd 6: K6, kfbf, k18, kfbf, k8, kfbf, k18, kfbf, k2—64 sts.

Rnd 8: K7, kfbf, k20, kfbf, k10, kfbf, k20, kfbf, k3—72 sts.

Rnd 10: K8, kfbf, k22, kfbf, k12, kfbf, k22, kfbf, k4—80 sts.

Rnd 12: K9, kfbf, k24, kfbf, k14, kfbf, k24, kfbf, k5—88 sts.

Rnd 14: K10, kfbf, k26, kfbf, k16, kfbf, k26, kfbf, k6—96 sts.

BO loosely in purl. Fasten off.

TIP
The construction technique used for the Tindra Herringbone Scarf (page 114) would also work well with this, or any rectangular, motif.

STARBURST CIRCLE

CO 11 sts using knitted CO (see Glossary).

Rows 1–2: K9, turn, k9.

Rows 3–4: K7, turn, k7.

Rows 5–6: K5, turn, k5.

Rows 7–8: K3, turn, k3.

Row 9: K3, BO 5, k3.

Row 10: K3, KCO 5, k3.

Rows 11–12: K11, turn, k11.

Rows 13–96: Rep Rows 1–12 six more times.

With another needle, pick up 11 sts along the original CO row. Holding original CO edge and last row together, BO using three-needle BO technique (see Glossary). Fasten off.

STARBURST SQUARE

CO 11 sts using knitted CO (see Glossary).

Rows 1–2: K9, turn, k9.

Rows 3–4: K7, turn, k7.

Rows 5–6: K5, turn, k5.

Rows 7–8: K3, turn, k3.

Row 9: K3, BO 5, k3.

Row 10: K3, CO 5 sts using knitted CO, k3.

Rows 11–12: K11, turn, k11.

Rows 13–144: Rep Rows 1–12 eleven more times.

With another needle, pick up 11 sts along the original petal CO row. Then holding original CO edge and last row together, BO using three-needle BO technique (see Glossary).

Using a long tail and tapestry needle, sew lines across the opening in a starburst design. Make an extra wrap around the center to solidify it. Fasten off.

TIP
See what a difference yarn makes by comparing this swatch knit in a worsted-weight yarn to the motifs in the Zuna Starburst Shrug, which are stitched in a lightweight brushed alpaca yarn.

(as featured in Zuna Starburst Shrug, page 82)

XOOX CABLED TILE

CO 26 sts.

Rows 1 and 2: Knit.

Row 3: (RS) K2, p3, k16, p3, k2.

Row 4 (and all even-numbered rows): (WS) K5, p16, k5.

Row 5: K2, p3, C4F, C4B, C4B, C4F, p3, k2.

Row 7: K2, p3, k16, p3, k2.

Row 9: K2, p3, C4B, C4F, C4F, C4B, p3, k2.

Row 11: Rep Row 7.

Row 13: Rep Row 9.

Row 15: Rep Row 7.

Row 17: Rep Row 5.

Row 19: Rep Row 3.

Rows 20 and 21: Knit.

BO loosely in knit. Fasten off.

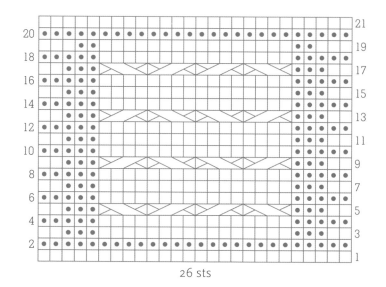

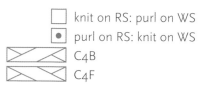

	knit on RS: purl on WS
	purl on RS: knit on WS
	C4B
	C4F

26 sts

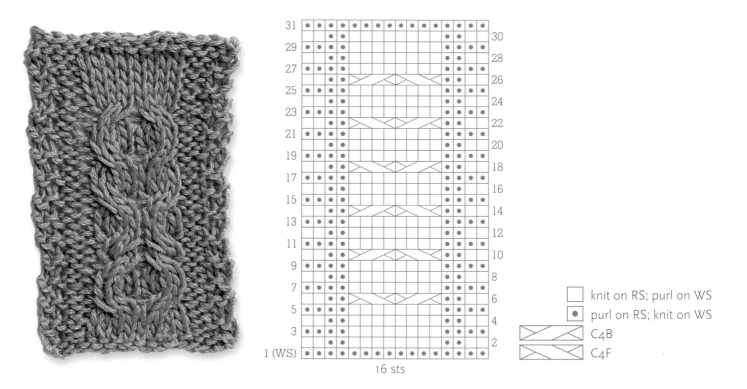

		knit on RS; purl on WS
•		purl on RS; knit on WS
		C4B
		C4F

16 sts

OXO CABLED TILE

CO 16 sts.

Row 1: Knit.

Row 2: (RS) K2, p2, k8, p2, k2.

Row 3 (and all odd-numbered rows): (WS) K4, p8, k4.

Row 4: Rep Row 3.

Row 6: K2, p2, C4B, C4F, p2, k2.

Row 8: Rep Row 3.

Row 10: K2, p2, C4F, C4B, p2, k2.

Row 12: Rep Row 3.

Row 14: K2, p2, C4F, C4B, p2, k2.

Row 16: Rep Row 3.

Row 18: K2, p2, C4B, C4F, p2, k2.

Row 20: Rep Row 3.

Row 22: K2, p2, C4B, C4F, p2, k2.

Row 24: Rep Row 3.

Row 26: K2, p2, C4F, C4B, p2, k2.

Row 28: Rep Row 3.

Row 30: Rep Row 3.

Row 31: Knit. BO all sts kwise.

TIP
Swap this motif for some or all of the motifs in
the Tindra Herringbone Scarf (page 114) for
an easy variation.

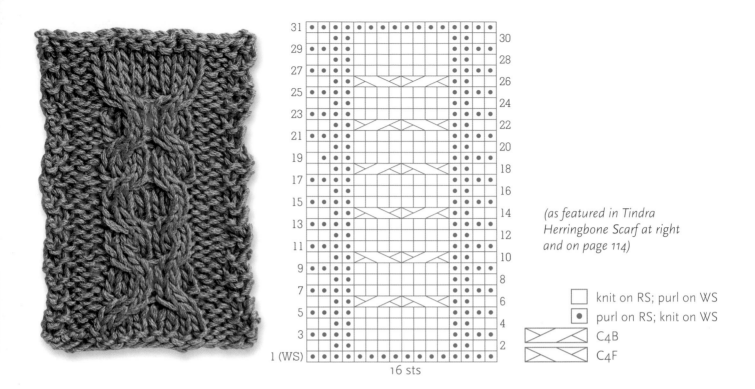

(as featured in Tindra Herringbone Scarf at right and on page 114)

☐	knit on RS; purl on WS
☐•	purl on RS; knit on WS
⬦	C4B
⬦	C4F

16 sts

XOX CABLED TILE

CO 16 sts.

Row 1: Knit.

Row 2: (RS) K2, p2, k8, p2, k2.

Row 3 (and all odd-numbered rows): (WS) K4, p8, k4.

Row 4: Rep Row 3.

Row 6: K2, p2, C4F, C4B, p2, k2.

Row 8: Rep Row 3.

Row 10: K2, p2, C4B, C4F, p2, k2.

Row 12: Rep Row 3.

Row 13: K2, p2, C4B, C4F, p2, k2.

Row 16: Rep Row 3.

Row 18: K2, p2, C4F, C4B, p2, k2.

Row 20: Rep Row 3.

Row 22: K2, p2, C4F, C4B, p2, k2.

Row 24: Rep Row 3.

Row 26: K2, p2, C4B, C4F, p2, k2.

Row 28: Rep Row 3.

Row 30: Rep Row 3.

Row 31: Knit.

BO all sts kwise.

TIP
Take the construction method used for the Tindra Herringbone Scarf and expand it to create a richly textured baby blanket or throw using this motif or the OXO Cabled Tile on page 41. The irregular edging will add an interesting design element.

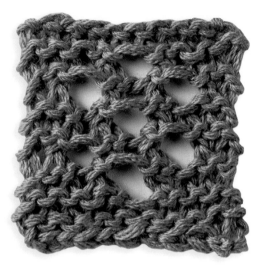

(as featured in Siri Möbius Cowl, page 78)

LACY SQUARE

CO 10 sts.

Row 1: Knit.

Row 2: Knit.

Row 3: K3, k2tog, yo twice, ssk, k3.

Row 4 (and all even-numbered rows through 12): Knit across, knitting into the front and the back of any double yo on previous row so that you end with a total of 10 sts.

Row 5: K1, (k2tog, yo twice, ssk) 2 times, k1.

Row 7: Rep Row 3.

Row 9: Rep Row 5.

Row 11: Rep Row 3.

Row 13: Rep Row 1.

Row 14: Knit.

BO all sts.

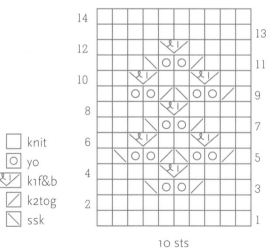

	knit
O	yo
⊻	k1f&b
╱	k2tog
╲	ssk

10 sts

GARTER-STITCH SQUARE WITH DIAMOND LACE CENTER

(as featured in Kiara Tile-Edged Shawl, page 94)

CO 20 sts.

Rows 1–6: Knit.

Row 7: K8, k2tog, yo twice, ssk, k8.

Row 8: K9, knit into the front and back of double yo on prev row, k8.

Row 9: K7, k2tog, yo, k2, yo, ssk, k7.

Row 10: Knit.

Row 11: K6, k2tog, yo, k4, yo, ssk, k6.

Row 12: Knit.

Row 13: K5, k2tog, yo, k6, yo, ssk, k5.

Row 14: Knit.

Row 15: K4, k2tog, yo, k2, k2tog, yo twice, ssk, k2, yo, ssk, k4.

Row 16: Rep Row 8.

Row 17: Rep Row 13.

Row 18: Knit.

Row 19: Rep Row 11.

Row 20: Knit.

Row 21: Rep Row 9.

Row 22: Knit.

Row 23: Rep Row 7.

Row 24: Rep Row 8.

Rows 25–30: Knit.

BO all sts.

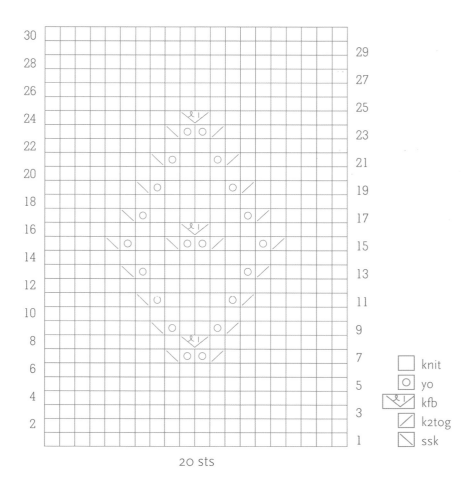

20 sts

☐	knit
○	yo
⧖	kfb
╱	k2tog
╲	ssk

SHORT-ROW CABLE-EDGED RING

CO 25 sts (13 sts for short-rows + 12 sts for cable section).

Row 1: (K1, p1) 6 times, k12 (leaving last st unworked).

Row 2: K12, (k1, p1) 6 times.

Row 3: (K1, p1) 6 times, k11 (leaving rem sts unworked).

Row 4: K11, (k1, p1) 6 times.

Row 5: 4/4LC, (k1, p1) 2 times, k10 (leaving rem sts unworked).

Row 6: K10, (k1, p1) 6 times.

Row 7: (K1, p1) 6 times, k9 (leaving rem sts unworked).

Row 8: K9, (k1, p1) 6 times.

Row 9: (K1, p1) 6 times, k8 (leaving rem sts unworked).

Row 10: K8, (k1, p1) 6 times.

Row 11: (K1, p1) 2 times, 4/4RC, k7 (leaving rem sts unworked).

Row 12: K7, (K1, p1) 6 times.

Row 13: (K1, p1) 6 times, k6 (leaving rem sts unworked).

Row 14: K6, (k1, p1) 6 times.

Row 15: (K1, p1) 6 times, k5 (leaving rem sts unworked).

Row 16: K5, (k1, p1) 6 times.

Row 17: 4/4LC, (k1, p1) 2 times, k4 (leaving rem sts unworked).

Row 18: K4, (k1, p1) 6 times.

Row 19: (K1, p1) 6 times, k3 (leaving rem sts unworked).

Row 20: K3, (k1, p1) 6 times.

Row 21: (K1, p1) 6 times, k2 (leaving rem sts unworked).

Row 22: K2, (k1, p1) 6 times.

Row 23: (K1, 1p) 2 times, 4/4RC, k13.

Row 24: K13, (k1, p1) 6 times.

Rep Rows 1–24 for pattern 5 more times.

BO loosely in pattern. Sew seam.

TIP
Sew two circles together and add a handle to create a fun bag, or cast on more stitches to create larger circles for a pillow. As an alternative to sewing the circles, crochet them together with a contrasting yarn for an unexpected detail.

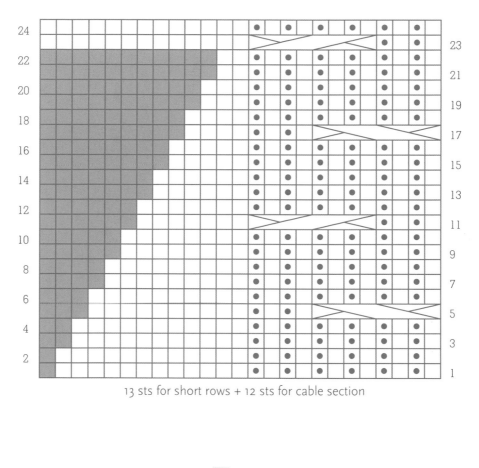

13 sts for short rows + 12 sts for cable section

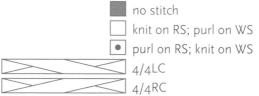

no stitch

knit on RS; purl on WS

purl on RS; knit on WS

4/4LC

4/4RC

SPIRAL CIRCLE

Using dpn, CO 6 sts, join to work in the round. Divide sts over 3 or 4 dpn, join without twisting, and pm for beg of rnd.

Rnd 1: K1f&b 6 times—12 sts.

Rnd 2 (and all even-numbered rnds): Knit.

Rnd 3: (K1, yo) 12 times—24 sts.

Rnd 5: (K2, yo) 12 times—36 sts.

Rnd 7: (K3, yo) 12 times—48 sts.

Rnd 9: (K4, yo) 12 times—60 sts.

Rnd 11: (K5, yo) 12 times—72 sts.

Rnd 13: (K6, yo) 12 times—84 sts.

Rnd 15: (K7, yo) 12 times—96 sts.

Rnd 16: Purl.

BO loosely in knit. Fasten off.

TIP
This motif would make a lovely center for the crown of a beret. Skip Rnd 16 and continue in pattern until you have the desired size, then begin decreasing toward the brim.

SWISS DOT CIRCLE

Rnd 1: Using dpn, make a slipknot, (k1, yo) 5 times, k1f&b all in same loop—12 sts. Divide sts over 4 dpn, join without twisting, and pm for beg of rnd.

Rnd 2: Knit.

Rnd 3: K1f&b in each st around—24 sts.

Rnd 4: Knit.

Rnd 5: *K3, yo 3 times, k3. Rep from * around.

Rnd 6: *K3, (k1, p1, k1, p1, k1) in yo on prev rnd, dropping extra loops, k3. Rep from * around—44 sts.

Rnds 7–10: Knit.

Rnd 11: *Yo 3 times, k11. Rep from * around.

Rnd 12: *(K1, p1, k1, p1, k1) in yo on prev rnd, dropping extra loops, k11—64 sts.

Rnds 13–16: Knit.

Rnd 17: *K8, yo 3 times, k5, yo 3 times, k3. Rep from * around.

Rnd 18: *K8, (k1, p1, k1, p1, k1) in yo on prev rnd, dropping extra loops, k5, (k1, p1, k1, p1, k1) in yo on prev rnd, dropping extra loops, k3. Rep from * around—104 sts.

Rnds 19–22: Knit.

Rnd 23: Purl.

Rnd 24: Knit.

Rnd 25: Purl.

BO loosely in knitting as follows: K1, *yo, k1. Insert LH needle into yo and first st and pass both loops up, over second st, and off needles. Rep from * around. Fasten off.

TULIP-LACE SQUARE

Using dpn, make slipknot, knit into the front and back of loop until you have 8 sts. Divide sts over 3 or 4 dpn, join without twisting, and pm for beg of rnd.

Rnd 1: K1f&b in each st around.

Rnd 2 (and all even-numbered rnds): Knit.

Rnd 3: *K1, yo, k3, yo. Rep from * around—24 sts.

Rnd 5: *K1, yo, k2tog, yo, k1, yo, ssk, yo. Rep from * around—32 sts.

Rnd 7: *K1, yo, k2tog, k1, yo, k1, yo, k1, ssk, yo. Rep from * around—40 sts.

Rnd 9: *K1, yo, k2tog, k2, yo, k1, yo, k2, ssk, yo. Rep from * around—48 sts.

Rnd 11: *K1, yo, k2tog, k3, yo, k1, yo, k3, ssk, yo. Rep from * around—56 sts.

Rnd 13: *K1, yo, k2tog, k4, yo, k1, yo, k4, ssk, yo. Rep from * around—64 sts.

Rnd 15: *K1, yo, k2, k2tog, yo, ssk, k1, yo, k1, yo, k1, k2tog, yo, ssk, k2, yo. Rep from * around—72 sts.

Rnd 17: *K1, yo, k2, k2tog, yo, k1, yo, ssk, k3, k2tog, yo, k1, yo, ssk, k2, yo. Rep from * around—80 sts.

Rnd 19: *K1, yo, k7, yo, ssk, k1, k2tog, yo, k7, yo. Rep from * around—88 sts.

Rnd 21: *K1, yo, k9, yo, s2kp, yo, k9, yo. Rep from * around.

Rnd 23: Knit.

Rnd 25: BO in purl as follows: P1, *yo, p1, pass yo and first st up and over second st and off needle. Rep from * around. Fasten off.

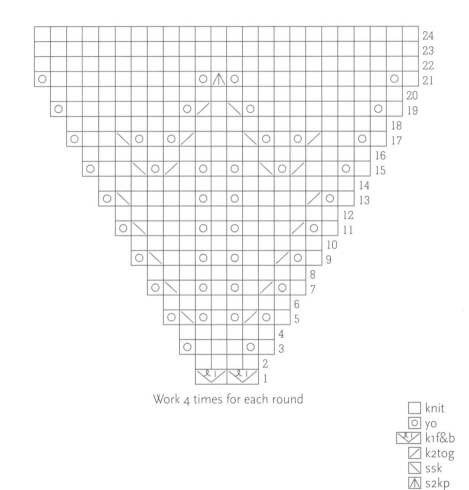

Work 4 times for each round

□ knit
◉ yo
⊻ k1f&b
╱ k2tog
╲ ssk
⋀ s2kp

EYELET SQUARE

Using dpn, make slipknot, (k1, p1) 6 times—12 sts. Divide sts over 3 or 4 dpn, join without twisting, and pm for beg of rnd.

Rnd 1: Knit.

Rnd 2: *Yo, k2, yo, k1. Rep from * around—20 sts.

Rnd 3 (and all odd-numbered rnds): Knit.

Rnd 4: *Yo, k1, yo, k2tog, k1, yo, k1. Rep from * around—28 sts.

Rnd 6: *Yo, k1, (yo, k2tog) 2 times, k1, yo, k1. Rep from * around—36 sts.

Rnd 8: *Yo, k3, yo, k2tog, k3, yo, k1. Rep from * around—44 sts.

Rnd 10: *Yo, k1, yo, k2tog, k4, yo, k2tog, k1, yo, k1. Rep from * around—52 sts.

Rnd 12: *Yo, k1, (yo, k2tog,) 2 times, k2, (yo, k2tog) 2 times, k1, yo, k1. Rep from * around—60 sts.

Rnd 14: *Yo, k3, yo, k2tog, k4, yo, k2tog, k3, yo, k1. Rep from * around—68 sts.

Rnd 16: *Yo, k1, (yo, k2tog, k4) 2 times, yo, k2tog, k1, yo, k1. Rep from * around—76 sts.

Rnd 18: *Yo, k1, (yo, k2tog, k2) 2 times, (yo, k2tog) 2 times, k1, yo, k1. Rep from * around—84 sts.

Rnd 20: *Yo, k3, (yo, k2tog, k4) 2 times, yo, k2tog, k3, yo, k1. Rep from * around—92 sts.

Rnd 22: *Yo, k22, yo, k1. Rep from * around—100 sts.

Rnd 23: Purl.

Rnd 24: *Yo, k24, yo, k1. Rep from * around—108 sts.

Rnd 25: Purl. BO loosely as follows: K1, *yo, k1. Pass yo and first st up and over second st and off needles. Rep from * until last st. Fasten off.

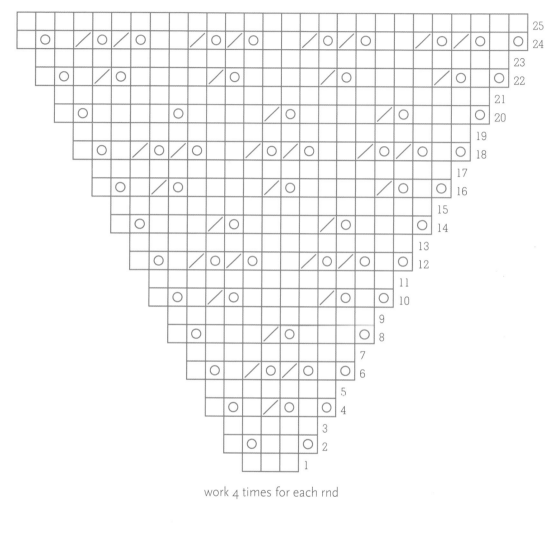

work 4 times for each rnd

☐ knit
🔘 yo
⧄ k2tog

Join–as–You–Go Motifs

These motifs are some of my favorites to knit, and I used them in several projects. As you knit each motif, you join it to the last motif you made to form continuous strips that can be used as is or combined with multiple strips to create larger areas of fabric. The best part is that no seaming is required!

(as featured in Mia Brioche-Stitch Scarf at right and on page 98)

GARTER-STITCH TRIANGLES

First Triangle

CO 19 sts.

*K10, turn, k2, turn, k3, turn, k4, turn, k5, turn, k6, turn, k7, turn, k8, turn, k9, turn, k10, turn, k11, turn, k12, turn, k13, turn, k14, turn, k15, turn, k16, turn, k17, turn, k18, turn, k19. BO 18 sts, leaving 1 st on needle.

Second Triangle

CO 18 sts for a total of 19 sts. Rep from * to complete the next triangle.

Continue until you have the desired number of triangle motifs. BO all sts.

TIP
To add a beautiful scalloped hem to a shawl, skirt, or other garment, pick up and knit a multiple of 19 stitches around the entire edge then follow the pattern without casting on additional stitches.

GARTER-STITCH DIAMONDS

Diamond Shaping

CO 19 sts.

K10, turn, k2, turn, k3, turn, k4, turn, k5, turn, k6, turn, k7, turn, k8, turn, k9, turn, k10, turn, k11, turn, k12, turn, k13, turn, k14, turn, k15, turn, k16, turn, k17, turn, k18, turn, k19, turn, k18, turn, k17, turn, k16, turn, k15, turn, k14, turn, k13, turn, k12, turn, k11, turn, k10, turn, k9, turn, k8, turn, k7, turn, k6, turn, k5, turn, k4, turn, k3, turn, k2, turn, k10.

Single Diamond

CO 19 sts. Turn. Work diamond shaping. Turn, bind off all sts.

First Strip

CO 19 sts. *Turn and work diamond shaping. Turn, bind off all sts except the last st; CO 18 sts—19 sts. Rep from * until you have the desired number of diamonds; turn, bind off all sts.

Second and Subsequent Strips

To attach a second row of diamonds to a previously created row: CO 19 sts. *Turn and work diamond shaping. Turn, bind off 9 sts; pick up a stitch from the point of a diamond on the previous row and knit it together with the next st, bind off sts until one st remains; CO 18 sts—19 sts. Rep from * until you have the desired number of diamonds; turn, bind off all sts.

(as featured in Lynnea Argyle-Lace Pullover, page 102)

ARGYLE DIAMONDS

First Diamond

CO 1 st.

Row 1: Kfbf—3 sts.

Rows 2, 4, 8, 10, 12, 14, 16, 20, 22: Knit.

Row 3: K1f&b, k1, k1f&b—5 sts.

Row 5: K1f&b, k3, k1f&b, CO 5 sts using knitted CO (see Glossary), BO 5 sts —7 sts.

Row 6: Knit across, CO 5 sts using knitted CO, BO 5 sts.

Row 7: K1f&b, k5, k1f&b—9 sts.

Row 9: K1f&b, k7, k1f&b—11 sts.

Row 11: K1f&b, k9, k1f&b—13 sts.

Row 13: Ssk, k9, k2tog—11 sts.

Row 15: Ssk, k7, k2tog—9 sts.

Row 17: Ssk, k5, k2tog, CO 5 sts using knitted CO, BO 5 sts—7 sts.

Row 18: Knit across, CO 5 sts using knitted CO, BO 5 sts—7 sts.

Row 19: Ssk, k3, k2tog—5 sts.

Row 21: Ssk, k1, k2tog—3 sts.

Row 23: S2kp—1 st.

Second and Subsequent Diamonds

Row 1: Kfbf—3 sts.

Rows 2, 4, 8, 10, 12, 14, 16, 20, 22: Knit.

Row 3: K1f&b, k1, k1f&b—5 sts.

Row 5: K1f&b, k3, k1f&b, CO 4 sts, pick up and knit (see Glossary) in tip of 5-st strip at end of row 17 of prev motif, BO 5 sts—7 sts.

Row 6: K7, CO 4 sts, pick up and knit in tip of 5-st strip at end of row 18, BO 5 sts.

Row 7: K1f&b, k5, k1f&b—9 sts.

Row 9: K1f&b, k7, k1f&b—11 sts.

Row 11: K1f&b, k9, k1f&b—13 sts.

Row 13: Ssk, k9, k2tog—11 sts.

Row 15: Ssk, k7, k2tog—9 sts.

Row 17: Ssk, k5, k2tog, CO 5, BO 5—7 sts.

Row 18: K7, CO 5 sts, BO 5 sts.

Row 19: Ssk, k3, k2tog—5 sts.

Row 21: Ssk, k1, k2tog—3 sts.

Row 23: S2kp—1 st.

Fasten off.

(as featured in Thora Lace Cardigan at right and on page 120)

MINI MEDALLIONS

Using dpn, CO 3 sts; do not join.

Row 1: (RS) K1f&b, yo, k2—5 sts.

Rows 2, 4, 6, 8, 10: (WS) Knit.

Row 3: K2, yo, k1, yo, k2—7 sts.

Row 5: K2, yo, k3, yo, k2—9 sts.

Row 7: K1, ssk, yo, s2kp, yo, k2tog, k1—7 sts.

Row 9: K1, ssk, yo, k3tog, k1—5 sts.

Row 11: Ssk, k1, k2tog—3 sts.

Row 12: S2kp—1 st.

Row 13: Knit into the front, back, and front of the same st—3 sts.

Row 14: Rep Row 2.

First Strip

Rep Rows 1–14 until you have desired number of medallions. End last medallion at Row 12. Fasten off.

Second Strip

*Rep Rows 1–5 of first medallion, pick up and knit along edge of adjacent medallion on first strip. For Row 6, knit picked-up st and first st tog, knit across—9 sts. Rep Rows 7–14 of first medallion. Rep from * until you have the desired number of medallions in this strip, but end last one at Row 12. Fasten off.

Third and Subsequent Strips

*Rep Rows 1–5 of first medallion, pick up and knit along edge of adjacent medallion on second strip. For Row 6, knit picked-up st and first st tog, knit across—9 sts. Rep Rows 7–14 of first medallion. Rep from * until you have the desired number of medallions in this strip, but end last one at Row 12. Fasten off.

Unusual Shapes

Circles and squares aren't the only geometric shapes you can knit. Triangles, pentagons, hexagons, and infinity shapes are a bit more challenging to combine but they create stunning designs. Have fun playing with different arrangements to see what you come up with.

STOCKINETTE-STITCH TRIANGLE

Using dpn, make slipknot and knit into front and back of loop until you have 6 sts. Divide sts over 3 dpn, join without twisting, and pm for beg of rnd.

Rnd 1: Knit—6 sts.

Rnd 2: *(K1, yo, k1) in same st, k1. Rep from * around—12 sts.

Rnd 3 (and all odd-numbered rnds): Knit.

Rnd 4: *K1, (k1, yo, k1) in same st, k2. Rep from * around—18 sts.

Rnd 6: *K2, (k1, yo, k1) in same st, k3. Rep from * around—24 sts.

Rnd 8: *K3, (k1, yo, k1) in same st, k4. Rep from * around—30 sts.

Rnd 10: *K4, (k1, yo, k1) in same st, k5. Rep from * around—36 sts.

BO loosely in purl. Fasten off.

STOCKINETTE-STITCH PENTAGON

Using dpn, make slipknot and knit into front and back of loop until you have 10 sts. Divide sts over 3 or 4 dpn, join without twisting, and pm for beg of rnd.

Rnd 1 (and all odd-numbered rnds): Knit.

Rnd 2: *Yo, k1. Rep from * around—20 sts.

Rnd 4: *K1, yo, k1, yo, k2. Rep from * around—30 sts.

Rnd 6: *K2, yo, k1, yo, k3. Rep from * around—40 sts.

Rnd 8: *K3, yo, k1, yo, k4. Rep from * around—50 sts.

Rnd 10: *K4, yo, k1, yo, k5. Rep from * around—60 sts.

BO loosely in purl. Fasten off.

> **TIP**
> Attach multiple pentagons point-side down to the edge of a shawl or a skirt hem for an interesting jagged edging. Seam the sides of the pentagons together or leave them loose for extra movement.

STOCKINETTE-STITCH HEXAGON

Using dpn, make slipknot and knit into front and back of loop until you have 12 sts. Divide sts over 3 or 4 dpn, join without twisting, and pm for beg of rnd.

Rnd 1: Knit 12 sts.

Rnd 2: *K1, yo twice, k1. Rep from * around.

Rnd 3: *K1, knit into front and back of yo on prev round, dropping extra loop, k1. Rep from * around—24 sts.

Rnd 4: *K2, yo twice, k2. Rep from * around.

Rnd 5: *K2, knit into front and back of yo on prev round, dropping extra loop, k2. Rep from * around—36 sts.

Rnd 6: *K3, yo twice, k3. Rep from * around.

Rnd 7: *K3, knit into front and back of yo on prev round, dropping extra loop, k3. Rep from * around—48 sts.

Rnd 8: *K4, yo twice, k4. Rep from * around.

Rnd 9: *K4, knit into front and back of yo on prev round, dropping extra loop, k4. Rep from * around—60 sts.

Rnd 10: *K5, yo twice, k5. Rep from * around.

Rnd 11: *K5, knit into front and back of yo on prev round, dropping extra loop, k5. Rep from * around—72 sts.

BO loosely in purl. Fasten off.

> **TIP**
> Combine hexagons to create a honeycomb fabric that can be left flat or joined into a tube for an easy cowl.

HEXAGON WITH CHAIN EDGING

Using dpn, CO 12 sts. Divide sts over 4 dpn, join without twisting, and pm for beg of rnd.

Rnd 1 (and all odd-numbered rnds): Knit.

Rnd 2: *K1, (k1, yo, k1) in next st. Rep from * around—24 sts.

Rnd 4: *K2, (k1, yo, k1) in next st, k1. Rep from * around—36 sts.

Rnd 6: *K3, (k1, yo, k1) in next st, k2. Rep from * around—48 sts.

Rnd 8: *K4, (k1, yo, k1) in next st, k3. Rep from * around—60 sts.

Rnd 10: *K5, (k1, yo, k1) in next st, k4. Rep from * around—72 sts.

Rnd 11: Knit.

BO as follows: Sl 2, k2tog, p2sso, chain-2 BO (see Glossary) 9 times. *Sl 2, k2tog, p3sso, chain-2 BO 9 times. Rep from * around. Insert needle into first st at beg of round, pick up a st, pass last chain over and fasten off—18 loops.

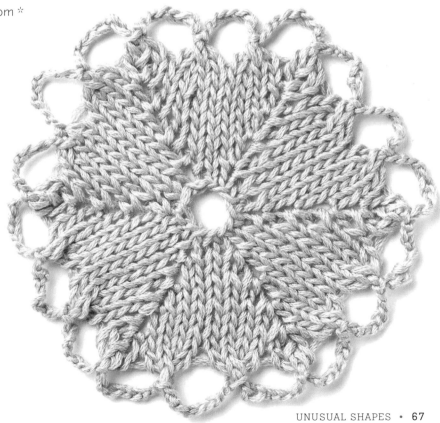

MEDALLION WITH CHAIN EDGING

Using dpn, make a slipknot, knit into the front of the loop, then knit into the back of the loop 6 times—12 sts. Divide sts over 3 dpn, join without twisting, and pm for beg of rnd.

Rnd 1: Knit.

Rnd 2: K1f&b 12 times—24 sts.

Rnds 3–4: Knit.

Rnd 5: *K1f&b, k1. Rep from * around—36 sts.

Rnds 6–7: Knit.

Rnd 8: *K1f&b, k2. Rep from * around—48 sts.

Rnds 9–10: Knit.

BO as follows: Slip 2 sts, k2tog, pass 2 sl sts over. *Chain-2 BO (see Glossary) 9 times, slip next 2 sts on row to RH needle (3 loops on RH needle), k2tog, pass 3 sts over. Rep from * around, chain-2 BO 9 times, pick up and knit into first dec st at beg of round, pass loop over, fasten off—12 ch-9 loops.

(as featured in Shania Medallion Hat at right and on page 86)

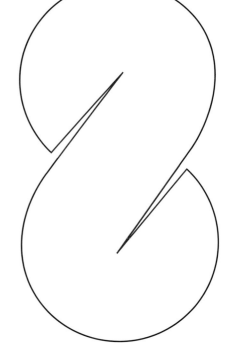

ASSEMBLY DIAGRAM
Sew side edges to cast-on and
bind-off edges along red lines.

GARTER-STITCH
INFINITY LOOP

CO 43 sts.

Row 1: (RS) (K2tog, k4) 6 times, k6, k1f&b 3 times in last st—42 sts.

Row 2 (and all even-numbered rows): (WS) Knit.

Row 3: (K2, k2tog, k1) 6 times, k6, k1f&b 6 times—42 sts.

Row 5: (K2, k2tog) 6 times, k6, (k1f&b, k1) 6 times.

Row 7: (K2tog, k1) 6 times, k6, (k1, k1f&b, k1) 6 times.

Row 9: K2tog 6 times, k6, (k3, k1f&b) 6 times.

Row 11: Sl 3, k3tog, p2sso, (k1f&b, k4) 6 times.

Row 12: Knit across to last 2 sts; k2tog.

BO all sts loosely.

Sew 2 ends to sides to form the infinity-loop shape.

TIP
In an infinity loop, one side starts with zero stitches in the repeats and the other side starts with the largest number of stitches in the repeats. One side increases up and the other decreases down. To enlarge an infinity motif, cast on more stitches in a multiple of the stitch pattern and increase or decrease according to the pattern.

STOCKINETTE-STITCH INFINITY LOOP

CO 71 sts.

Row 1: (RS) (K2tog, k8) 6 times, k10, k1f&b 3 times in last st—70 sts.

Row 2 (and all even-numbered rows): (WS) Purl.

Row 3: (K2, k2tog, k5) 6 times, k10, (M1, k1) 6 times—70 sts.

Row 5: (K6, k2tog) 6 times, k10, (k1, M1, k1) 6 times—70 sts.

Row 7: (K2tog, k5) 6 times, k10, (k3, M1) 6 times—70 sts.

Row 9: (K2, k2tog, k2) 6 times, k10, (M1, k4) 6 times.

Row 11: (K3, k2tog) 6 times, k10, (k3, M1, k2) 6 times.

Row 13: (K1, k2tog, k1) 6 times, k10, (k6, M1) 6 times.

Row 15: (K2tog, k1) 6 times, k10, (k4, M1, k3) 6 times.

Row 17: K2tog 6 times, k10, (M1, k8) 6 times.

Row 19: Sl 3, k3tog, p3sso, k10, (k5, M1, k4) 6 times.

Row 20: Purl across to last 2 sts; p2tog.

BO all sts loosely.

Sew 2 ends to sides to form infinity-loop shape.

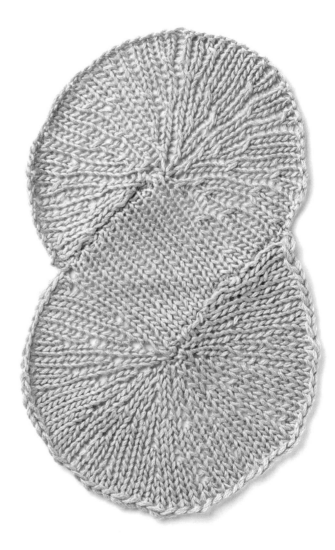

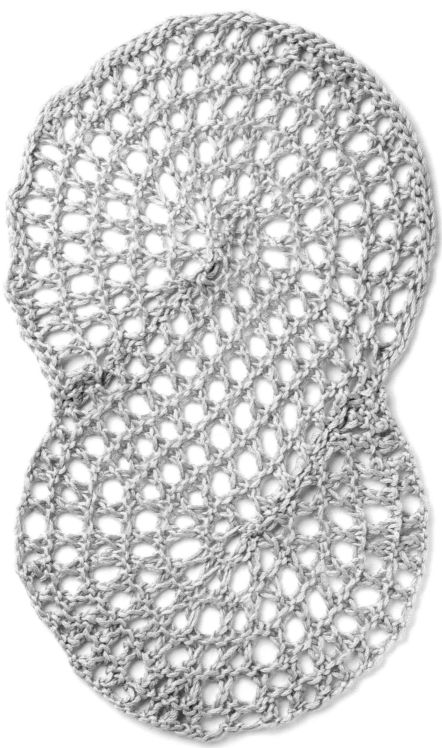

EYELET-LACE INFINITY LOOP

CO 85 sts.

Row 1: (RS) (K2tog, k10) 6 times, k12, k1f&b 3 times in last st—84 sts.

Row 2: (WS) K1, *(yo, k2tog). Rep from * across to last st, k1.

Row 3: (K2, k2tog, k7) 6 times, k12, (k1f&b) 6 times—84 sts.

Row 4: Knit.

Row 5: (K6, k2tog, k2) 6 times, k12, (k1f&b, k1) 6 times—84 sts.

Row 6: Rep Row 2.

Row 7: (K2tog, k7) 6 times, k12, (k1, k1f&b, k1) 6 times—84 sts.

Row 8: Knit.

Row 9: (K2, k2tog, k4) 6 times, k12, (k3, k1f&b) 6 times—84 sts.

Row 10: Rep Row 2.

Row 11: (K3, k2tog, k2) 6 times, k12, (k1f&b, k4) 6 times—84 sts.

Row 12: Knit.

Row 13: (K1, k2tog, k3) 6 times, k12, (k3, k1f&b, k2) 6 times—84 sts.

Row 14: Rep Row 2.

Row 15: (K2tog, k3) 6 times, k12, (k6, k1f&b) 6 times—84 sts.

Row 16: Knit.

Row 17: (K1, k2tog, k1) 6 times, k12, (k4, k1f&b, k3) 6 times—84 sts.

Row 18: Rep Row 2.

Row 19: (K1, k2tog) 6 times, k12, (k8, k1f&b) 6 times—84 sts.

Row 20: Knit.

Row 21: (K2tog) 6 times, k12, (k3, k1f&b, k6) 6 times—84 sts.

Row 22: Rep Row 2.

Row 23: Sl 3, k3tog, p3sso, k12, (k1f&b, k10) 6 times—85 sts.

Row 24: Knit across to last 2 sts; k2tog.

BO all sts loosely.

Sew 2 ends to side to form infinity-loop shape.

TIP

Infinity loops are nontraditional motifs that are actually quite versatile. I have joined infinity loops in strips for a scarf or rectangular shawl and used one as the back of a cardigan. To incorporate an infinity loop into a garment, pick up and knit all around the outside edge of the loop and continue knitting to create your desired shape.

RIDGED DIAMOND

CO 3 sts.

Row 1: (RS) K1, k1f&bf, k1—5 sts.

Row 2: (WS) K2, p1, k2.

Row 3: K1, k1f&b, k1, k1f&b, k1—7 sts.

Row 4: K2, p3, k2.

Row 5: K1, k1f&b, k3, k1f&b, k1—9 sts.

Row 6: K2, p5, k2.

Row 7: K1, k1f&b, k5, k1f&b, k1—11 sts.

Row 8: K2, p7, k2.

Row 9: K1, k1f&b, k7, k1f&b, k1—13 sts.

Row 10: K2, p9, k2.

Row 11: K1, k1f&b, k9, k1f&b, k1—15 sts.

Row 12: Knit.

Row 13: K1, k1f&b, k11, k1f&b, k1—17 sts.

Row 14: K2, p13, k2.

Row 15: K1, k1f&b, k13, k1f&b, k1—19 sts.

Row 16: K2, p15, k2.

Row 17: K1, k1f&b, k15, k1f&b, k1—21 sts.

Row 18: K2, p17, k2.

Row 19: K1, k1f&b, k17, k1f&b, k1—23 sts.

Row 20: K2, p19, k2.

Row 21: K1, k1f&b, k19, k1f&b, k1—25 sts.

Row 22: Knit.

Row 23: K1, k1f&b, k21, k1f&b, k1—27 sts.

Row 24: K2, p23, k2.

Row 25: K1, k1f&b, k23, k1f&b, k1—29 sts.

Row 26: K2, p25, k2.

Row 27: K1, k1f&b, k25, k1f&b, k1—31 sts.

Row 28: K2, p27, k2.

Row 29: K1, k1f&b, k27, k1f&b, k1—33 sts.

Row 30: K2, p29, k2.

Row 31: K1, k1f&b, k29, k1f&b, k1—35 sts.

Row 32: Knit.

Row 33: K1, k2tog, k29, ssk, k1—33 sts.

Row 34: K2, p29, k2.

Row 35: K1, k2tog, k27, ssk, k1—31 sts.

Row 36: K2, p27, k2.

Row 37: K1, k2tog, k25, ssk, k1—29 sts.

Row 38: K2, p25, k2.

Row 39: K1, k2tog, k23, ssk, k1—27 sts.

Row 40: K2, p23, k2.

Row 41: K1, k2tog k21, ssk, k1—25 sts.

Row 42: Knit.

Row 43: K1, k2tog, k19, ssk, k1—23 sts.

Row 44: K2, p19, k2.

Row 45: K1, k2tog, k17, ssk, k1—21 sts.

Row 46: K2, p17, k2.

Row 47: K1, k2tog, k15, ssk, k1—19 sts.

Row 48: K2, p15, k2.

Row 49: K1, k2tog, k13, ssk, k1—17 sts.

Row 50: K2, p13, k2.

Row 51: K1, k2tog, k11, ssk, k1—15 sts.

Row 52: Knit.

Row 53: K1, k2tog, k9, ssk, k1—13 sts.

Row 54: K2, p9, k2.

Row 55: K1, k2tog, k7, ssk, k1—11 sts.

Row 56: K2, p7, k2.

Row 57: K1, k2tog, k5, ssk, k1—9 sts.

Row 58: K2, p5, k2.

Row 59: K1, k2tog, k3, ssk, k1—7 sts.

Row 60: K2, p3, k2.

Row 61: K1, k2tog, k1, ssk, k1—5 sts.

Row 62: K2, p1, k2.

Row 63: K1, s2kp, k1—3 sts.

Row 64: K3tog.

Fasten off.

RUFFLED DIAMOND

Create a Ridged Diamond following instructions at left. On any of the purl bump rows on the right side (Rows 12, 22, 32, 42, 52), working in either the n-shaped bumps or the u-shaped bumps, work as follows: Pick up and knit (see Glossary) into garter ridge loop, *yo, pick up and knit into the next same-shaped garter ridge loop. Rep from * across. Knit 8 rows. BO as follows: K1, *yo, k1. Pass yo and first st up and over second st and off needles. Rep from * across to last st. Fasten off.

TIP
Join multiple ruffled diamonds to create a fabulously fluffy pillow or afghan. Turn the diamonds in different directions to vary the angle of the ruffles.

The Projects

This mini collection of projects showcases just a few of the many motifs in this book and the myriad ways in which they can be used. I've created several scarves, shawls, other accessories, and sweaters to demonstrate the creative possibilities of using motifs. Use them as starting points for your own designs!

Siri Möbius Cowl

THE MÖBIUS CAST-ON IS A FUN TECHNIQUE that creates a twisted loop—perfect for an extra-long cowl. Lacy square motifs add an unusual texture and flair to an otherwise simple knit fabric. The edging is worked perpendicularly to the edge of the live stitches, and you bind off the final round as you go, simultaneously making the edging and binding off for a seamless project.

Finished Size

14" (35.5 cm) length by 56" (142 cm) circumference.

Yarn

Sport weight (#2 Fine).
Shown here: Bijou Spun Bijou Bliss (50% yak, 50% cormo wool; 150 yd [137 m]/56 g): #04 blush, 2 skeins.

Needles

Size U.S. 8 (5 mm): 32" (81.5 cm) circular (cir).
Adjust needle size if necessary to obtain the correct gauge.

Notions

Tapestry needle.

Gauge

12 sts and 16 rows = 4" (10 cm) in St st.
Lacy Square motif = 3" (7.5 cm) square.

Note

The edging of the cowl is based on the Lacy Square motif (see page 44).

Cowl

CO 160 sts using Möbius CO (see Glossary).

Rnd 1: Knit around—320 sts.

Rnds 2–8: Rep Rnd 1.

Rnd 9: Purl around—320 sts.

Rnds 10–16: Rep Rnd 9.

BO as follows: *BO 4 sts, CO 4 sts using knitted CO (see Glossary), pick up and knit into last BO st on RH needle, BO 5 sts (forms scalloped picot), BO 4 sts along Row 16. Rep from * around.

NOTE: *You finish the BO edge between a repeat of the scalloped picots. This is because you won't need to fasten off and begin again for the square motif edging.*

SQUARE MOTIF

Keeping the final st from completing the Möbius BO edge, CO 9 sts—10 sts.

Row 1: K10.

Row 2: Knit.

Row 3: K3, k2tog, yo twice, ssk, k3.

Row 4 (and all even-numbered rows through 12): Knit across, knitting into the front and the back of any double yo on previous row so that you end with a total of 10 sts.

Row 5: K1, (k2tog, yo twice, ssk) 2 times, k1.

Row 7: Rep Row 3.

Row 9: Rep Row 5.

Row 11: Rep Row 3.

Row 13: Rep Row 1.

Row 14: Knit across.

**BO 9 sts, (1 st should remain on needle), CO 9 sts using knitted CO, pick up and knit 1 st on Möbius edge halfway between next 2 picots.

Row 1: K2tog, k across—10 sts.

Row 2 (and all even-numbered rows through 12): Knit across, knitting into the front and the back of any double yo on previous row.

Row 3: K3, k2tog, yo twice, ssk, k3.

Row 5: K1, (k2tog, yo twice, ssk) 2 times, k1.

Row 7: Rep Row 3.

Row 9: Rep Row 5.

Row 11: Rep Row 3.

Row 13: Rep Row 1.

Row 14: Knit across.

Rep from ** 38 more times.

BO 9 sts, pick up and knit into corner of first motif, BO together.

Fasten off.

Finishing

Weave in ends. Steam block or wet block, and drape on a dress form.

> **TIP**
> Any square motif worked in rows could be used as an edging for this cowl. Because the corner of the motif is joined to the cowl, the number of stitches in the motif is not critical.

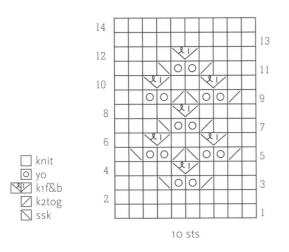

knit
yo
k1f&b
k2tog
ssk

10 sts

Zuna Starburst Shrug

FOUR SQUARE MOTIFS ARE JOINED to create the back of this dreamy wrap. Stitches are then picked up all around the back and knit into a wide ribbed border, forming the structure of the shrug. The brushed baby alpaca yarn is so light and gauzy it reminds me of cotton candy. Wear it over your favorite dress for just a touch of warmth and an ethereal effect.

Finished Size
About 36 (38, 40)" (91.5 [96.5, 101.5] cm) bust circumference. Shown in size 36" (91.5 cm).

Yarn
DK weight (#3 Light).
Shown here: The Alpaca Yarn Company Halo (78% Suri alpaca, 22% nylon; 514 yd [470 m]/50 g): #7967 green, 1 (1, 1) ball.

Needles
Size U.S. 8 (5 mm): 24" (61 cm) circular (cir).
Adjust needle size if necessary to obtain the correct gauge.

Notions
Tapestry needle.

Gauge
Each motif is 7½ (8, 8½)" (19, 20.5, 21.5 cm) square, after blocking.

Note
The shrug is based on the Starburst Square motif (see page 39).

Shrug

MOTIF (MAKE 4)

CO 11 (12, 13) sts using knitted CO (see Glossary).

Rows 1–2: K9 (10, 11), turn, k9 (10, 11).

Rows 3–4: K7 (7, 8), turn, k7 (7, 8).

Rows 5–6: K5 (5, 5), turn, k5 (5, 5).

Rows 7–8: K3 (3, 3), turn, k3 (3, 3).

Row 9: K3, BO 5 (5, 6), k3.

Row 10: K3, CO 5 (5, 6) sts using knitted CO method, k3.

Rows 11–12: K11 (12, 13), turn, k11 (12, 13).

Rows 13–144: Rep Rows 1–12 eleven more times.

With another needle, pick up 11 (12, 13) sts along the original petal CO row. Then, holding original CO edge and last row together, BO using three-needle BO technique (see Glossary). Using a long tail and tapestry needle, sew lines across the opening in a starburst design. Make an extra wrap to solidify the center. Fasten off. Block each motif to finished measurements before assembly.

ASSEMBLY

Holding 2 motifs together with right sides facing, pick up and knit 30 sts along one side through both thicknesses. Do not break yarn. Holding the next 2 motifs together with right sides facing, pick up and knit 30 sts along one side through both thicknesses—60 sts.

BO all sts loosely.

With right sides facing, and working along other interior edge of motifs, pick up and knit 30 sts through both thicknesses of 2 motifs, then pick up and knit 30 sts through both thicknesses of last 2 motifs—60 sts.

BO all sts loosely.

BORDER

Rnd 1: With right side facing, beginning at any corner, pick up and knit 72 sts evenly across each side of square grid of 4 motifs joined together—288 sts.

Rnd 2: *K3, p3. Rep from * around.

Rnds 3–4: Rep Rnd 2.

Rnd 5: P1f&b, (k1, p1) in next st, k1f&b in next st, (p3, k3) 11 times, *p1f&b, (p1, k1) in next st, k1f&b in next st, p1f&b in next st, (p1, k1) in next st, k1f&b in next st, (p3, k3) 11 times. Rep from * 2 more times, p1f&b, (p1, k1) in next st, k1f&b—312 sts.

Rnd 6: *P3, k3. Rep from * around.

Rnds 7–10: Rep Rnd 6.

Rnd 11: *P3, k3. Rep from * 12 more times. BO next 78 sts. *P3, k3. Rep from * 12 more times. BO last 78 sts. Join in a round to finish lower edge—156 sts.

Rnd 12: *P3, k3. Rep from * around.

Rnds 13–20: Rep Rnd 12.

Rnd 21: *P3, k1, k1f&b, k1. Rep from * around—182 sts.

Rnds 22–30: *P3, k4. Rep from * around.

BO loosely. Fasten off.

Finishing

Weave in loose ends. Block to measurements.

> ### TIP
> Gauge is important for this type of project, of course, but any square motif could work. Try using one large square or nine smaller squares.

Shania Medallion Hat

....

INSPIRED BY A TILED GARDEN FLOOR and origami folding, this hat is an exploration of joining motifs to create a fabric, then "bending" the two-dimensional fabric to create a three-dimensional fabric: the crown of a hat. I love how the color striping in this yarn makes beautiful starbursts in the center of the medallions and also creates subtle striping in the ribbed brim.

Finished Size

21" (53.5 cm) circumference (unstretched);
7½" (19 cm) deep.

Yarn

Sport weight (#2 Fine).
Shown here: Lorna's Laces Sportmate (70% superwash merino, 30% Outlast viscose; 270 yd [247 m]/100 g): watercolor, 1 hank.

Needles

Size U.S. 6 (4 mm): set of 4 or 5 double-pointed (dpn).
Size U.S. 3 (3.25 mm): 16" (40.5 cm) circular (cir) or longer if using magic loop method.
Adjust needle size(s) if necessary to obtain the correct gauge.

Notions

Tapestry needle; stitch marker.

Gauge

Each motif is 3" (7.5 cm) in diameter (not including chain edging), after blocking, using size U.S. 6 (4 mm) dpn.
20 sts and 36 rnds = 4" (10 cm) in k2, p2 ribbing, after blocking, using size U.S. 3 (3.25 mm) circular.

Notes

- The crown of the hat is based on the Medallion with Chain Edging motif (see page 68).
- All sl sts in this pattern should be slipped as if to knit.

Hat

FIRST MOTIF

With dpn, make a slipknot, then make 12 sts by knitting into the front of the loop, then knitting into the back of the loop 6 times—12 sts.

Separate sts onto 3 dpn (4 sts per dpn) and join in the round, being careful to not twist sts, pm to mark beginning of round.

Rnd 1: Knit.

Rnd 2: K1f&b 12 times—24 sts.

Rnds 3–4: Knit.

Rnd 5: *K1f&b, k1. Rep from * around—36 sts.

Rnds 6–7: Knit.

Rnd 8: *K1f&b, k2. Rep from * around—48 sts.

Rnds 9–10: Knit.

BO as follows: Slip 2 sts, k2tog, pass 2 sl sts over. *Chain-2 BO (see Glossary) 9 times, slip next 2 sts on row to right-hand needle (3 loops on RH needle), k2tog, pass 3 sts over. Rep from * around, chain-2 BO 9 times, pick up and knit into first dec st at beg of round, pass loop over, fasten off—12 ch9 loops.

SECOND MOTIF

Rep first motif through Rnd 10.

BO as follows: Slip 2 sts, k2tog, pass 2 sl sts over. *Chain-2 BO 4 times, insert needle into ch9 opening on adjacent motif and chain-2 BO (to join the 2 motifs together), chain-2 BO 4 times, slip next 2 sts on row to right-hand needle (3 loops on RH needle), k2tog, pass 3 sts over. Rep from * 3 more times. **Chain-2 BO 9 times, slip next 2 sts on row to right-hand needle (3 loops on RH needle), k2tog, pass 3 sts over. Rep from ** 7 more times, chain-2 BO 9 times, pick up and knit into first dec st at beg of round, pass loop over, fasten off—12 ch9 loops (4 of which are joined to adjacent motif).

THIRD THROUGH FIFTH MOTIFS

Rep second motif, making sure to join to previous motif in the correct loops (see diagram).

SIXTH MOTIF

NOTE: *The sixth motif joins the strip of motifs into a tube, so it is joined to first motif on one side and fifth motif on the opposite side.*

Rep first motif through Rnd 10.

BO as follows: Slip 2 sts, k2tog, pass 2 sl sts over. *Chain-2 BO 4 times, insert needle into ch9 opening on adjacent motif (Motif 5) and chain-2 BO (to join the 2 motifs together), chain-2 BO 4 times, slip next 2 sts on row to right-hand needle (3 loops on RH needle), k2tog, pass 3 sts over. Rep from * 3 more times. **Chain-2 BO 9 times, slip next 2 sts on row to right-hand needle (3 loops on RH needle), k2tog, pass 3 sts over. Rep from ** 1 more time (2 unattached chains). Rep from * 4 more times, but joining to Motif 1. Rep from ** 2 more times, chain-2 BO 9 times, pick up and knit into first dec st at beg of round, pass loop over, fasten off—12 ch9 loops (4 of which are joined to Motif 5 and 4 of which are joined to Motif 1).

NOTE: *The six motifs are joined into a loop.*

HAT BRIM

Using circular needle, pick up and knit 4 sts into each chain opening around 1 edge of the 6 motifs—96 sts.

Rnd 1: *K2, p2. Rep from * around.

Rep Rnd 1 until brim measures 3" (7.5 cm). BO in pattern. Fasten off.

CROWN MOTIF

NOTE: *The seventh (Crown) motif is joined to all the previous motifs with 2 ch9 loops per motif.*

Connecting Motifs

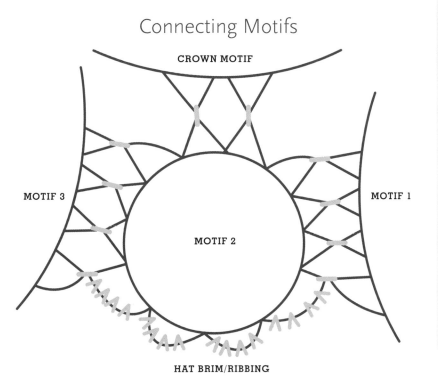

CROWN MOTIF

MOTIF 3

MOTIF 1

MOTIF 2

HAT BRIM/RIBBING

Rep first motif through Rnd 10.

BO as follows: Slip 2 sts, k2tog, pass 2 sl sts over. *Chain-2 BO 4 times, insert needle into ch9 opening on Motif 1 and chain-2 BO (to join the 2 motifs together), chain-2 BO 4 times, slip next 2 sts on row to right-hand needle (3 loops on RH needle), k2tog, pass 3 sts over. Rep from * once more for Motif 1, then rep from * 2 more times for Motifs 2, 3, 4, 5, and 6 for a total of 12 joined loops. Pick up and knit into first dec st at beg of round, pass loop over. Fasten off.

Finishing

Weave in loose ends. Block to finished measurements.

> **TIP**
> The Hexagon with Chain Edging motif (page 67) would make an easy substitute and create a subtly different effect.

Selena Crescent Moon Shawlette

THIS FLIRTY WRAP FEATURES AN UNUSUAL construction method; the "edging" is actually knit first. Eleven picot-edged half-circles are knit separately in stockinette stitch, then stitches are picked up to join them and begin the garter stitch "base" of the shawlette. The motifs are knit in a yarn the same color as the base but with tiny glass beads for a subtle sparkle.

Finished Size
30" (76 cm) long by 8½" (21.5 cm) wide [at widest point].

Yarn
Worsted weight (#4 Medium).
Shown here: Tilli Tomas Aspen (100% merino; 260 yd [238 m]/100 g): saffron, 1 hank (A).

Worsted weight (#4 Medium).
Shown here: Tilli Tomas Flurries (80% merino, 20% beads; 70 yd [64 m]/50 g): saffron, 2 hanks (B).

Needles
Size U.S. 8 (5 mm): 24" (61 cm) circular (cir).
Adjust needle size if necessary to obtain the correct gauge.

Notions
Tapestry needle.

Gauge
18 sts and 24 rows = 4" (10 cm) in St st.

Note
The edging of the shawlette is based on the Crescent Moon motif (see page 34).

Crescent Moon Motif (make 11)

With yarn B, CO 7 sts.

Row 1: K1f&b in each st across—14 sts.

Row 2: K1f&b in each st across—28 sts.

Row 3: Knit across.

Row 4: Purl across.

Rows 5–12: Rep Rows 3–4.

Picot BO as follows: *CO 3 sts using knitted CO (see Glossary), BO 6 sts. Rep from * across, CO 3 sts using knitted CO, BO 3 sts. Fasten off.

Shawlette

Row 1: *Working along flat edges of Crescent Moon motif rows, and with the right side facing you and using yarn A, pick up and knit 5 sts into side of first motif, CO 5 sts using knitted CO in the open U shape in top center of motif, pick up and knit 5 sts into other edge of rows on same motif**, CO 5 sts before next motif. Rep from * 9 more times, rep from * to ** once more—215 sts.

Row 2: Knit across.

Row 3: K10, turn.

Row 4: K10, turn.

Row 5: K15, turn.

Row 6: K20, turn.

Rows 7–43: Continue in established pattern, knitting 5 more sts on each row until you have knit across all 215 sts.

Row 44: Knit across—215 sts.

BO as follows: *CO 3 sts using knitting CO, BO 8 sts. Rep from * until 1 st remains. CO 3 sts, BO all sts. Fasten off.

Finishing

Weave in ends. Block to measurements.

TIP

If you fold a circular motif in half and offset it a bit so the shorter side is facing you, you could use the same construction method to create a tiered edging.

Kiara Tile-Edged Shawl

A SIMPLE TRIANGULAR SHAWL KNIT in a laceweight cashmere and silk yarn provides an ideal base for any number of edging options. The shawl is knit first, and the individual motifs are knit as extensions of the final row. I blocked the motifs to emphasize the diamond lace pattern in the center of each, and I couldn't resist adding a delicate bow to each end of the shawl for an extra feminine touch.

Finished Size

27" (68.5 cm) long by 32" (81.5 cm) wide, not including edging, after blocking.

Yarn

Fingering weight (#0 Lace).
Shown here: Fiesta Yarns Gracie's Lace (70% extrafine merino, 15% cashmere, 15% silk; 960 yd [878 m]/100 g): tahiti, 1 skein.

Needles

Size U.S. 8 (5 mm): 24" (61 cm) or 32" (81.5 cm) circular (cir) and 2 double-pointed (dpn) for motifs.
Adjust needle size if necessary to obtain the correct gauge.

Notions

Tapestry needle; stitch marker.

Gauge

32 sts and 32 rows = 4" (10 cm) in garter st, after blocking.

Note

Edging of shawl is based on the Garter-Stitch Square with Diamond Lace Center motif (see page 45).

Shawl

CO 5 sts using knitted CO (see Glossary).

Knit 10 rows.

Row 1: K5, yo, pick up and knit 5 sts along side edge of strip, yo, pick up and knit into free loops of all 5 CO sts—17 sts.

Row 2: K5, pm, (yo, k1, yo) in yo on prev row, pm, k5, pm, (yo, k1, yo) in yo on prev row, pm, k5—21 sts.

Row 3 (and all odd-numbered rows): Knit.

Row 4: K5, yo, k3, yo, k5, yo, k3, yo, k5—25 sts.

Row 6: K5, yo, k5, yo, k5, yo, k5, yo, k5—29 sts.

Row 8: K5, yo, k7, yo, k5, yo, k7, yo, k5—33 sts.

Row 10: K5, yo, k9, yo, k5, yo, k9, yo, k5—37 sts.

Rows 11–49: Continue in established pattern—113 sts.

Row 50: K5, yo, (k3, k1f&b) 12 times, k1, yo, k5, yo, (k3, k1f&b) 12 times, k1, yo, k5—141 sts.

Row 52: K5, yo, k63, yo, k5, yo, k49, yo, k5—145 sts.

Row 54: K5, yo, k65, yo, k5, yo, k51, yo, k5—149 sts.

Rows 55–77: Continue in established pattern—193 sts.

Row 78: K5, yo, (k3, k1f&b) 22 times, k1, yo, k5, yo, (k3, k1f&b) 22 times, k1, yo, k5—241 sts.

Row 80: K5, yo, k113, yo, k5, yo, k113, yo, k5—245 sts.

Row 82: K5, yo, k115, yo, k5, yo, k115, yo, k5—249 sts.

Row 84: K5, yo, k117, yo, k5, yo, k117, yo, k5—253 sts.

Rows 85–113: Continue in established pattern—309 sts.

Row 114: K5, yo, (k12, k1f&b) 11 times, k4, yo, k5, yo, (k12, k1f&b) 11 times, k4, yo, k5—335 sts.

Row 116: K5, (yo, k2tog) 80 times, k5, (yo, k2tog) 80 times, k5—335 sts.

Row 117: Knit across.

Next row: Knit across the first 5 sts; turn. Continue knitting these 5 sts for 20 rows. BO these sts.

Reattach yarn and knit across the next 20 sts; turn. Follow the edging motif instructions for Rows 2–30. BO.

Reattach yarn and work 7 more edging motifs over the next 140 sts.

Reattach yarn and k5 sts; turn. K these sts for 20 rows. BO.

Reattach yarn and work 8 more edging motifs over the next 160 sts.

Reattach yarn and k5 sts; turn. K these sts for 20 rows. BO.

EDGING MOTIF

Rows 1–6: Working over 20 sts, knit.

Row 7: K8, k2tog, yo twice, ssk, k8.

Row 8: K9, knit into the front and back of double yo on previous row, k8.

Row 9: K7, k2tog, yo, k2, yo, ssk, k7.

Row 10: Knit across.

Row 11: K6, k2tog, yo, k4, yo, ssk, k6.

Row 12: Rep Row 10.

Row 13: K5, k2tog, yo, k6, yo, ssk, k5.

Row 14: Rep Row 10.

Row 15: K4, k2tog, yo, k2, k2tog, yo twice, ssk, k2, yo, ssk, k4.

Row 16: Rep Row 8.

> **TIP**
> Any square or rectangular motif that is worked in rows could be substituted for the one I used here. If you use a motif with more than 20 stitches, use fewer motifs; if you choose one with less then 20 stitches, just increase the number to fit.

Row 17: Rep Row 13.

Row 18: Rep Row 10.

Row 19: Rep Row 11.

Row 20: Rep Row 10.

Row 21: Rep Row 9.

Row 22: Rep Row 10.

Row 23: Rep Row 7.

Row 24: Rep Row 8.

Rows 25–30: Knit.

Bind off: K1, *yo, k1. Pass yo and second st up and over first st and off needle. Rep from * to last st. Fasten off.

Finishing

Weave in ends. Block to measurements.

Construction Diagram

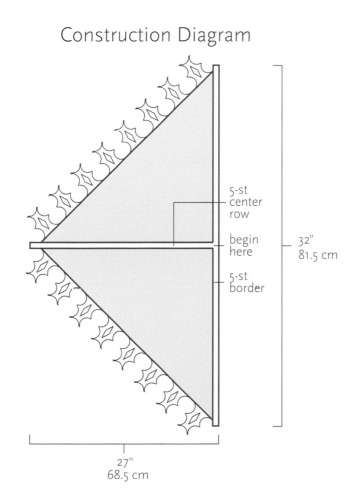

5-st center row

begin here

5-st border

32"
81.5 cm

27"
68.5 cm

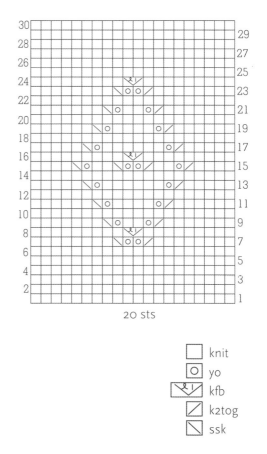

20 sts

☐ knit

⊡ yo

⊠ kfb

⊿ k2tog

◺ ssk

Mia Brioche-Stitch Scarf

INSPIRED BY A WALK ALONG THE BEACH, the feathery scallops on this scarf remind me of the layers of ripples created by wave after wave washing over the sand. I chose a brioche stitch for the base of the scarf because the prominent, raised ridges of stitches make a super-simple beginning for easily picking up stitches.

Finished Size
6" (15 cm) wide by 40" (101.5 cm) long.

Yarn
Sport weight (#2 Fine).
Shown here: Filatura Di Crosa/Tahki Stacy Charles, Inc. Zarina (100% extrafine merino; 181 yd [165 m]/50 g): #1935 aqua, 1 ball (MC).

Sport weight (#2 Fine).
Shown here: Filatura Di Crosa/Tahki Stacy Charles, Inc. Superior (70% cashmere, 25% schappe silk, 5% extrafine merino; 330 yd [300 m]/25 g): #55 light teal, 1 ball (CC1).

Fingering weight (#0 Lace).
Shown here: Filatura Di Crosa/Tahki Stacy Charles, Inc. Nirvana (100% extrafine merino; 372 yd [340 m]/25 g): #5 aqua, 1 ball (CC2).

Needles
Size U.S. 6 (4 mm) needles.
Adjust needle size if necessary to obtain the correct gauge.

Notions
Tapestry needle.

Gauge
18 sts and 20 rows = 4" (10 cm) in brioche stitch and MC, after blocking.

Note
Ruffles are based on Garter-Stitch Triangles motif (see page 56).

Scarf

NOTE: *Slip all sl sts as if to purl.*

With MC, CO 26 sts.

Set-up row: *Yo, sl 1, k1. Rep from * across.

Row 1: *Yo, sl, k2tog (yo and slip st from previous row). Rep from * across.

Rep row 1 until scarf is 40" (101.5 cm) long.

BO as follows: *K1, yo, k2tog. Pass yo and knit st up and over the k2tog st, *yo, k1, pass yo and 2nd to last st up and over the last st. Rep from * across.

RUFFLE
First ruffle

Working sideways along the elongated sl sts in a peak column and working in the seventh (middle) column, and using CC2, pick up and knit in first elongated sl st. *Yo, pick up and knit in next elongated sl st. Rep from * across—281 sts.

Row 2: Knit.

Row 3: **K11, turn, k2, turn, k3, turn, k4, turn, k5, turn, k6, turn, k7, turn, k8, turn, k9, turn, k10, turn, k11, turn, k12, turn, k13, turn, k14, turn, k15, turn, k18, turn, BO 20 sts *loosely* as follows: Yo, k1, pass yo and remaining k1 st over the last st. *Yo, k1, pass yo and 2nd to last up and over the last st. Repeat from * until 20 sts have been bound off. Do not fasten off. Rep from ** until entire row is bound off.

Second through fifth ruffles

Repeat as for first ruffle, but skip 2 ridges along surface of brioche scarf and pick up and knit into next (third) ridge, then into the edge column on each side of scarf base. Alternate petal ruffles in CC1 and CC2.

Finishing

Weave in ends. Block to measurements.

TIP

For this scarf, I used three yarns in different tones of the same color, but there are so many other possibilities, including complementary colors, three yarns in a single color, or just one yarn used throughout.

Lynnea Argyle-Lace Pullover

WATCHING A SPIDER GAVE ME THE IDEA for this pullover (you never know where you'll find inspiration!). Fascinated by the action of the spider weaving its web, I created motifs that are worked individually and joined in strips as you go to create the top of the sweater. The effect looks far more elaborate than the actual knitting construction. A knit-in tied belt adds another bit of feminine flair to this pretty-in-pink pullover.

Finished Sizes

About 32 (34, 38, 42, 48)" [81.5 (86.5, 96.5, 106.5, 122) cm] bust circumference. Shown in size 32" (81.5 cm).

Yarn

DK weight (#3 Light).
Shown here: Drew Emborsky Sarcastic (50% Peruvian cotton, 50% Tencel; 110 yd [100 m]/55 g): fer sure, 5 (6, 6, 7, 8) skeins.

Needles

Size U.S. 4 (3.5 mm) needles.
Size U.S. 4 (3.5 mm): 32" (81.5 cm) circular (cir).
Adjust needle size if necessary to obtain the correct gauge.

Notions

Stitch holders; tapestry needle.

Gauge

17 sts and 30 rows = 4" (10 cm) in garter st.

Notes

- Top section of pullover is based on the Argyle Diamonds motif (see page 59).
- Motif section is worked first, then body of sweater is worked from motifs down.

Motif Section

FIRST STRIP
First diamond motif

CO 1 st.

Row 1: Kfbf—3 sts.

Rows 2, 4, 8, 10, 12, 14, 16, 20, 22: Knit across.

Row 3: K1f&b, k1, k1f&b—5 sts.

Row 5: K1f&b, k3, k1f&b, CO 5 sts, BO 5 sts—7 sts.

Row 6: K7, CO 5 sts, BO 5 sts.

Row 7: K1f&b, k5, k1f&b—9 sts.

Row 9: K1f&b, k7, k1f&b—11 sts.

Row 11: K1f&b, k9, k1f&b—13 sts.

Row 13: Ssk, k9, k2tog—11 sts.

Row 15: Ssk, k7, k2tog—9 sts.

Row 17: Ssk, k5, k2tog, CO 5, BO 5—7 sts.

Row 18: K7, CO 5 sts, BO 5 sts—7 sts.

Row 19: Ssk, k3, k2tog—5 sts.

Row 21: Ssk, k1, k2tog—3 sts.

Row 23: S2kp—1 st.

Second diamond motif

＊**Row 1:** Kfbf—3 sts.

Rows 2, 4, 8, 10, 12, 14, 16, 20, 22: Knit across.

Row 3: K1f&b, k1, k1f&b—5 sts.

Row 5: K1f&b, k3, k1f&b, CO 4 sts, pick up and knit in tip of 5-st strip at end of row 17 of prev motif, BO 5 sts—7 sts.

Row 6: K7, CO 4 sts, pick up and knit in tip of 5-st strip at end of row 18, BO 5 sts.

Row 7: K1f&b, k5, k1f&b—9 sts.

Row 9: K1f&b, k7, k1f&b—11 sts.

Row 11: K1f&b, k9, k1f&b—13 sts.

Row 13: Ssk, k9, k2tog—11 sts.

Row 15: Ssk, k7, k2tog—9 sts.

Row 17: Ssk, k5, k2tog, CO 5 sts, BO 5 sts—7 sts.

Row 18: K7, CO 5 sts, BO 5 sts.

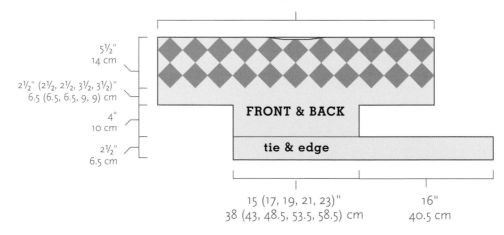

31 (33, 35, 37, 39)"
79 (84, 89, 94, 99) cm

5½"
14 cm

2½" (2½, 2½, 3½, 3½)"
6.5 (6.5, 6.5, 9, 9) cm

4"
10 cm

2½"
6.5 cm

FRONT & BACK

tie & edge

15 (17, 19, 21, 23)"
38 (43, 48.5, 53.5, 58.5) cm

16"
40.5 cm

Row 19: Ssk, k3, k2tog—5 sts.

Row 21: Ssk, k1, k2tog—3 sts.

Row 23: S2kp—1 st.

Rep from * 9 (10, 11, 12, 13) more times for a total of 10 (11, 12, 13, 14) motifs. Fasten off.

SECOND STRIP
First diamond motif

CO 1 st.

Row 1: Kfbf—3 sts.

Rows 2, 4, 8, 10, 14, 16, 20, 22: Knit across.

Row 3: K1f&b, k1, k1f&b—5 sts.

Row 5: K1f&b, k3, k1f&b, CO 4 sts, pick up and knit in 5-st

strip on adjacent strip's first motif, BO 5 sts—7 sts.

Row 6: K7, CO 5 sts, BO 5 sts.

Row 7: K1f&b, k5, k1f&b—9 sts.

Row 9: K1f&b, k7, k1f&b—11 sts.

Row 11: K1f&b, k9, k1f&b—13 sts.

Row 12: Pick up and knit 1 st in side of Row 12 on adjacent motif, slip st to left needle, k2tog, knit across—13 sts.

Row 13: Ssk, k9, k2tog—11 sts.

Row 15: Ssk, k7, k2tog—9 sts.

Row 17: Ssk, k5, k2tog, CO 4 sts, pick up and knit in 5-st strip on adjacent strip's motif, BO 5 sts—7 sts.

Row 18: K7, CO 5 sts, BO 5 sts—7 sts.

Row 19: Ssk, k3, k2tog—5 sts.

Row 21: Ssk, k1, k2tog—3 sts.

Row 23: S2kp—1 st.

Second diamond motif

*****Row 1:** Kfbf—3 sts.

Rows 2, 4, 8, 10, 14, 16, 20, 22: Knit across.

Row 3: K1f&b, k1, k1f&b—5 sts.

Row 5: K1f&b, k3, k1f&b, CO 4 sts, pick up and knit in tip of 5-st strip at end of Row 17 of prev motif.

BO 5 sts—7 sts.

Row 6: K7, CO 4 sts, pick up and knit in tip of 5-st strip at end of Row 18 and joined strips on adjacent strip simultaneously, BO 5 sts.

Row 7: K1f&b, k5, k1f&b—9 sts.

Row 9: K1f&b, k7, k1f&b—11 sts.

Row 11: K1f&b, k9, k1f&b—13 sts.

Row 12: Pick up and knit 1 st in side of Row 12 on

adjacent motif, slip st to left needle, k2tog, knit across—13 sts.

Row 13: Ssk, k9, k2tog—11 sts.

Row 15: Ssk, k7, k2tog—9 sts.

Row 17: Ssk, k5, k2tog, CO 4 sts, pick up and knit in tip of 5-st joined strips on adjacent strip, BO 5 sts—7 sts.

Row 18: K7, CO 5 sts, BO 5 sts.

Row 19: Ssk, k3, k2tog—5 sts.

Row 21: Ssk, k1, k2tog—3 sts.

Row 23: S2kp—1 st.

Rep from * 9 (10, 11, 12, 13) more times. Fasten off.

THIRD STRIP

Rep as for second strip, except attach at the first 9 (10, 11, 12, 13) points, then do not join the next 5 points (leaving neck hole opening), then attach at the next 9 (10, 11, 12, 13) points. Fasten off.

FOURTH STRIP

Rep second strip, but joining to third strip. Fasten off.

Body

NOTE: *The 11 (12, 13, 14, 15) motifs have a total of 23 (25, 27, 29, 31) points from which to pick up and knit 1 st.*

FRONT

**Row 1: *Pick up and knit 1 st in first point, CO 6 sts using knit CO, pick up and knit in next point. Rep from * across—155 (169, 183, 197, 211) sts.

Row 2: *K2tog, k5. Rep from * across to last 6 sts: K2tog, k4, k2tog—132 (144, 156, 168, 180) sts.

Knit 16 (16, 16, 22, 22) more rows.

Sleeve shaping

Knit the first 38 (40, 42, 43, 43) sts, turn. Knit 3 (3, 3, 5, 5) more rows over these first sts.*** Place these sts on st holder.

Place middle 56 (64, 72, 82, 94) sts on holder.

Knit 4 (4, 4, 6, 6) rows on rem 38 (40, 42, 43, 43) sts, place on holder.

BACK

To make the sweater back, working with the 23 (25, 27, 29, 31) points along the rem edge of the fourth row of motifs, rep the above front instructions between ✳✳ and ✳✳✳ (to end of first sleeve shaping). Place the 38 (40, 42, 43, 43) front sleeve sts on another needle, then BO front and back sleeve sts using three-needle BO.

Place middle 56 (64, 72, 82, 94) sts on holder.

Knit 4 (4, 4, 6, 6) rows on rem 38 (40, 42, 43, 43) sts. Place the 38 (40, 42, 43, 43) front sleeve sts on another needle, then BO front and back sleeve sts using three-needle BO.

LOWER BODY

Using circular needles and beginning at the seam of the left sleeve at the underarm, pick up and knit 4 (4, 4, 5, 5) sts along left sleeve underarm sts, knit 56 (64, 72, 82, 94) sts from back holder, pick up and knit 8 (8, 8, 10, 10) sts from right sleeve underarm, knit 56 (64, 72, 82, 94) sts from front holder, pick up and knit 4 (4, 4, 5, 5) sts at left sleeve underarm, pm—128 (134, 160, 184, 208) sts.

Rnd 2: Purl around.

Rnd 3: Knit around.

Rep Rnds 2–3 for 3" (7.5 cm).

Next row: K2tog, knit across to last 2 sts, k2tog, turn.

Next row: Knit across.

Rep last 2 rows for 1" (2.5 cm).

BO all sts loosely.

BOTTOM BORDER AND TIE

CO 16 sts.

Knit 120 rows.

Next row: K15, sl1, knit live st on last row of sweater, pass sl st over, turn.

Next row: Knit across.

Repeat these last 2 rows around the lower edge of the sweater. Knit an additional 120 rows.

BO.

Finishing

Weave in ends. Block to measurements.

Fiola Flower Shawl

I HAVE ALWAYS BEEN DRAWN TO CREATING FLOWERS and natural textures in knitting. Many floral motifs are worked in rounds, but this is an exploration of making flowers in rows on straight needles. This deceptively simple flower motif would be beautiful on its own as an embellishment to another project, but here it is magically transformed into a lacy fabric by joining the petals of your current flower to the petals of previously knit flowers. A perpendicular strip of fabric, which joins to the outer-edge petals as you go, ties it all together.

Finished Size

25" (63.5 cm) wide by 70" (178 cm) long, after blocking.
Edging: 5" (12.5 cm) wide, after blocking.
Motif: 8" (20.5 cm) by 8" (20.5 cm), after blocking.

Yarn

Worsted weight (#4 Medium).
Shown here: Trendsetter Yarns Tonalita (52% wool, 48% acrylic; 100 yd [91 m]/50 g): #2396 starry night, 9 balls.

Needles

Size U.S. 8 (5 mm) knitting needles.
Adjust needle size if necessary to obtain the correct gauge.

Notions

Tapestry needle.

Gauge

16 sts and 24 rows = 4" (10 cm) in blocked garter st.

Notes

- This project is based on the Short-Row Flower motif (see page 18).
- When joining multiple petals together, pick up and knit into the same space for a more cohesive and neater midpoint center.

Shawl

FIRST FLOWER
First petal

CO 13 sts using knitted CO (see Glossary).

Row 1: K13.

Row 2: K7, turn, k2, turn, k3, turn, k4, turn, k5, turn, k6, turn, k7, turn, k8, turn, k9, turn, k10, turn, k11, turn, k12, turn, k13.

Second petal

*CO 13 sts using knitted CO.

Row 1: K13.

Row 2: K7, turn, k2, turn, k3, turn, k4, turn, k5, turn, k6, turn, k7, turn, k8, turn, k9, turn, k10, turn, k11, turn, k12, turn, k13.

Rep from * 6 more times, for a total of 8 petals—104 sts.

Next row: K2tog across—52 sts.

Next row: K2tog across—26 sts.

Next row: *Yo 3 times, k2tog. Rep from * across—26 sts.

Next row: Drop extra loops for each yo st, k2tog across—13 sts.

*Pass second to last st up and over last st. Rep from * until only 1 st remains on needle. Fasten off, leaving long tail.

Connecting Motifs

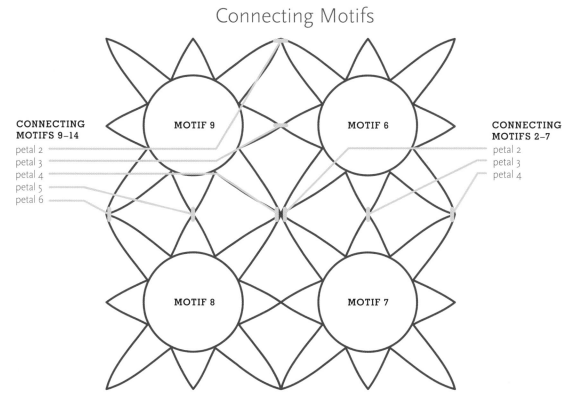

CONNECTING
MOTIFS 9–14

petal 2
petal 3
petal 4
petal 5
petal 6

MOTIF 9

MOTIF 6

CONNECTING
MOTIFS 2–7

petal 2
petal 3
petal 4

MOTIF 8

MOTIF 7

NINTH THROUGH FOURTEENTH FLOWERS

Attach the first, second, third, fourth, and fifth petals as shown in the diagram.

Finishing

Block the shawl at this point to get correct shape of flowers.

EDGING

CO 26 sts.

Row 1: K1, k2tog 2 times, k1f&b 4 times, k2tog 4 times, k1f&b 4 times, k2tog 2 times, k1.

Rows 2–3: Knit across.

Row 4: Rep Row 1.

Rows 5–6: Rep Row 2.

Row 7: Rep Row 1.

Row 8: Rep Row 2.

Row 9: BO 4 sts, knit across—22 sts.

Row 10: BO 4 sts, k6, BO 6 sts, k6.

Row 11: CO 4 sts, turn, k10, CO 6 sts, k6, CO 4 sts—26 sts.

SECOND THROUGH SEVENTH FLOWERS

Repeat for first flower, except when casting on for the first, second, and third petals, CO as follows: CO 6 sts using knitted CO, pick up and knit into adjacent flower's petal as shown on the diagram, CO 6 sts using knitted CO (for a total of 13 sts). Then proceed with original instructions for first flower.

EIGHTH FLOWER

Attach the first, second, and third petals to the side of the seventh flower, as shown in the diagram.

> **TIP**
> Try substituting other flower or star motifs with eight petals for the one used here, such as the Eight-Point Eyelet Star (page 17) or the Eight-Point Garter-Stitch Star (page 23). You might need to add or omit motifs if you want to keep the shawl the same size.

Row 12: K1, k1f&b 2 times, k2tog 4 times, k1f&b 4 times, k2tog 4 times, k1f&b 2 times, k1.

Rows 13–14: Rep Row 2.

Row 15: Rep Row 12.

Rows 16–17: Rep Row 2.

Row 18: Rep Row 12.

Row 19: Rep Row 2.

Row 20: K4, BO 6 sts, k6, BO 6 sts, k3, k2tog with last st and next flower petal on motifs to join edging to shawl.

Row 21: K4, CO 6sts, k6, CO 6 sts, k4.

Row 22: K1, k2tog 2 times, k1f&b 4 times, k2tog 4 times, k1f&b 4 times, k2tog 2 times, k1.

Joining Edging to Motifs

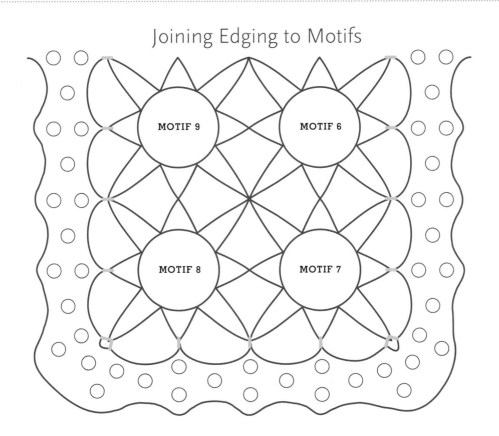

Rows 23–24: Knit across.

Row 25: Rep Row 1.

Rows 26–27: Rep Row 2.

Row 28: Rep Row 1.

Row 29: Rep Row 2.

Row 30: BO 4 sts, knit across—22 sts.

Row 31: BO 4 sts, k6, BO 6 sts, k6.

Row 32: CO 4 sts, turn, k10, CO 6 sts, k6, CO 4 sts—26 sts.

Row 33: K1, k1f&b 2 times, k2tog 4 times, k1f&b 4 times, k2tog 4 times, k1f&b 2 times, k1.

Rows 34–35: Rep Row 2.

Row 36: Rep Row 12.

Rows 37–38: Rep Row 2.

Row 39: Rep Row 12.

Row 40: Rep Row 2 to the last st, then k2tog with the last st and next flower petal on motifs to join edging to shawl.

Row 41: K4, BO 6 sts, k6, BO 6 sts, k4.

Row 42: K4, CO 6 sts, k6, CO 6 sts, k4.

Rep Rows 1–42, joining the edging to next flower petal on shawl at the ends of each Row 20 and 40. On corner petals, join twice (at two separate connection points) to create corner fullness.

Final row: BO all sts. Attach first 4 sts to first 4 sts of initial edging CO. Skip the next 6 sts, then attach middle 6 sts from edging CO and BO.

Weave in ends. Block to measurements.

Tindra Herringbone Scarf

THE CABLED TILES THAT MAKE UP THIS VIBRANT SCARF are embellished with knitted Xs and Os, symbolizing hugs and kisses. While the scarf would be beautiful knit in one color, I wanted to emphasize the herringbone texture created from the unique configuration of the tiles by using two shades of yellow. You might assume that the motif pieces are knit separately and sewn together, especially because they are knit in two separate colors—not so! Each new tile begins by picking up and knitting into the previous tile and, on the interior edge, joining as you go on every other row.

Finished Size
8½" (21.5 cm) wide by 30" (76 cm) long.

Yarn
Worsted weight (#4 Medium).
Shown here: Drew Emborsky Iconic (100% extrafine superwash merino; 120 yd [108 m]/55 g): banana seat, 1 skein (A); fondue, 1 skein (B).

Needles
Size U.S. 6 (4 mm) needles.
Adjust needle size if necessary to obtain the correct gauge.

Notions
Tapestry needle.

Gauge
Each motif is 3" (7.5 cm) by 5¼" (13.5 cm) after blocking.

Stitch Guide
C4B Slide 2 sts to cn and hold to the back of the work, k2, k2 from cn.

C4F Slide 2 sts to cn and hold to the front of the work, k2, k2 from cn.

Note
The scarf is based on the XOX Cabled Tile motif (see page 42).

Scarf

MOTIF 1

Row 1: CO 16 sts with color A.

Row 2: Knit across.

Row 3: K2, p2, k8, p2, k2.

Row 4 (and all even-numbered rows through Row 30): K4, p8, k4.

Row 5: Rep Row 3.

Row 7: K2, p2, C4F, C4B, p2, k2.

Row 9: Rep Row 3.

Row 11: K2, p2, C4B, C4F, p2, k2.

Row 13: Rep Row 3.

Row 15: K2, p2, C4B, C4F, p2, k2.

Row 17: Rep Row 3.

Row 19: K2, p2, C4F, C4B, p2, k2.

Row 21: Rep Row 3.

Row 23: K2, p2, C4F, C4B, p2, k2.

Row 25: Rep Row 3.

Row 27: K2, p2, C4B, C4F, p2, k2.

Row 29: Rep Row 3.

Row 31: Rep Row 3.

Row 32: Knit.

BO all sts kwise.

MOTIF 2

Row 1: With RS facing, pick up and knit 16 sts into the side of Motif 1 with color B, working evenly into each end of row. You should be joined to half of the length of the motif.

Rows 2–32: Rep Rows 2–32 of Motif 1.

BO all sts kwise.

MOTIF 3

Row 1: With RS facing, pick up and knit 16 sts into the side of Motif 2 with color A, working evenly into each end of row. You should be joined to half of the length of the motif. (See assembly diagram.)

Row 2: Knit across.

Row 3: K2, p2, k8, p2, k1, sl1, pick up and knit into next end of row in side of Motif 1.

Row 4: K2tog (using picked up st and sl st from end of last row), k3, p8, k4.

Row 5: Rep Row 3.

Row 6: Rep Row 4.

Row 7: K2, p2, C4F, C4B, p2, k1, sl1, pick up and knit into end of second next row in side of Motif 1.

Row 8: Rep Row 4.

Row 9: Rep Row 3.

Row 10: Rep Row 4.

Row 11: K2, p2, C4B, C4F, p2, k1, sl1, pick up and knit into end of second next row in side of Motif 1.

Row 12: Rep Row 4.

Row 13: Rep Row 3.

Row 14: Rep Row 4.

Row 15: K2, p2, C4B, C4F, p2, k1, sl1, pick up and knit into end of second next row in side of Motif 1.

Row 16: Rep Row 4.

Row 17: K2, p2, k8, p2 k2.

Row 18: K4, p8, k4.

Row 19: K2, p2, C4F, C4B, p2, k2.

Row 20: Rep Row 18.

Row 21: Rep Row 17.

Row 22: Rep Row 18.

Row 23: K2, p2, C4F, C4B, p2, k2.

Row 24: Rep Row 18.

Row 25: Rep Row 17.

Row 26: Rep Row 18.

Row 27: K2, p2, C4B, C4F, p2, k2.

Row 28: Rep Row 18.

Row 29: Rep Row 17.

Row 30: Rep Row 18.

Row 31: Rep Row 17.

Row 32: Knit.

BO all sts kwise.

Connecting Motifs

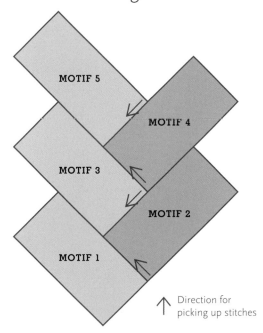

↑ Direction for picking up stitches

MOTIF 4

Row 1: With RS facing, pick up and knit 16 sts into the side of Motif 3 with color B, working evenly into each end of row. You should be joined to half of the length of the motif.

Row 2: Knit across to the last st; sl1, pick up and knit into next end of row in side of Motif 2.

Row 3: K2tog (using picked up st and sl st from end of last row), k1, p2, k8, p2, k2.

Row 4: K4, p8, k3, sl1, pick up and knit into next end of row in side of Motif 2.

Row 5: Rep Row 3.

Row 6: Rep Row 4.

Row 7: K2tog (using picked up st and sl st from end of last row), k1, p2, C4F, C4B, p2, k2.

Row 8: Rep Row 4.

Row 9: Rep Row 3.

Row 10: Rep Row 4.

Row 11: K2tog (using picked up st and sl st from end of last row), k1, p2, C4B, C4F, p2, k2.

Row 12: Rep Row 4.

Row 13: Rep Row 3.

Row 14: Rep Row 4.

Row 15: K2tog (using picked up st and sl st from end of last row), k1, p2, C4B, C4F, p2, k2.

Row 16: Rep Row 4.

Row 17: K2, p2, k8, p2, k2.

Row 18: K4, p8, k4.

Row 19: K2, p2, C4F, C4B, p2, k2.

Row 20: Rep Row 18.

Row 21: Rep Row 17.

Row 22: Rep Row 18.

Row 23: K2, p2, C4F, C4B, p2, k2.

Row 24: Rep Row 18.

Row 25: Rep Row 17.

Row 26: Rep Row 18.

Row 27: K2, p2, C4B, C4F, p2, k2.

Row 28: Rep Row 18.

Row 29: Rep Row 17.

Row 30: Rep Row 18.

Row 31: Rep Row 17.

Row 32: Knit.

BO all sts kwise.

Repeat the third and fourth motifs 10 more times each.

Finishing

Weave in ends. Block to measurements.

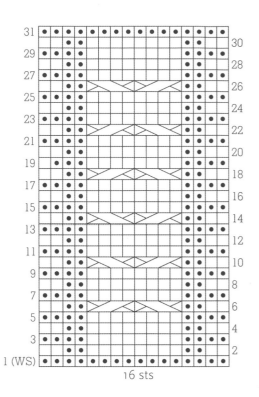

16 sts

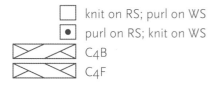

knit on RS; purl on WS

purl on RS; knit on WS

C4B

C4F

> **TIP**
> I left my design flat as a scarf, but it can be styled as a cowl with the addition of a pin, or you could create a tubular cowl by joining the last tiles to the first tiles at the beginning of the scarf.

Thora Lace Cardigan

I DESIGNED AND KNIT THIS CARDIGAN in the throes of a tropical rainstorm as I dreamt of brighter days and lush gardens. The top-down raglan-shaped yoke features a simple-to-remember lacy stitch pattern that reminds me of tiny flower petals. The openwork fabric around the wide collar features an eyelet medallion, symbolizing the sun and a hope for it to reemerge soon. And the final outer edging is simple garter stitch but binds off with a delicate picot edging reminiscent of tiny buds.

Finished Sizes

Cardigan at bust without motif edge: 32½ (35, 38, 42½, 44)" (82.5 [89, 96.5, 108, 112] cm).
Sample shown measures 32½" (82.5 cm).

Yarn

Sport weight (#2 Fine).
Shown here: Bijou Spun Lhasa Wilderness (75% yak, 25% bamboo; 180 yd [165 m]/56 g): #14 amethyst, 4 (5, 5, 6, 6) hanks.

Needles

Size U.S. 6 (4 mm): 24" (61 cm) or 32" (81.5 cm) circular (cir) and set of 4 or 5 double-pointed (dpn).
Adjust needle size if necessary to obtain the correct gauge.

Notions

Stitch holders (2) for holding sleeve stitches; stitch markers; tapestry needle.

Gauge

16 sts and 20 rows = 4" (10 cm) in lace pattern (from raglan yoke) after blocking.
Square medallions = 2" (5 cm) square, after blocking.

Notes

- Edging of cardigan is based on Mini Medallions motif (see page 60).
- In this pattern, the symbols { and } indicate the sts between the markers.

Yoke

CO 59 (65, 67, 71, 91) sts.

ALL SIZES

Row 1 (and all odd-numbered rows): (WS) Knit across.

Row 2: (RS) K2, pm, yo, k1 {left front}, yo, pm, k2, pm, yo, k3 (3, 3, 3, 5), yo, k3tog, yo, k3 (3, 3, 3, 5) {sleeve}, yo, pm, k2, pm, yo, [k3, yo, k3tog, yo] 4 (5, 6, 7, 8) times, k3 {back}, yo, pm, k2, pm, yo, k3 (3, 3, 3, 5), yo, k3tog, yo, k3 (3, 3, 3, 5) {sleeve}, yo, pm, k2, pm, yo, k1 {right front}, yo, pm, k2—69 (75, 77, 81, 101) sts.

Row 4: K2, yo, {k3}, yo, k2, yo, {k1 (1, 1, 1, 3), yo, k3tog, yo, k3, yo, k3tog, yo, k1 (1, 1, 1, 3)}, yo, k2, yo, {k1, [yo, k3tog, yo, k3] 4 (5, 6, 7, 8) times, yo, k3tog, yo, k1}, yo, k2, yo, {k1 (1, 1, 1, 3), yo, k3tog, yo, k3, yo, k3tog, yo, k1 (1, 1, 1, 3)}, yo, k2, yo, k3, yo, k2—79 (85, 87, 91, 111) sts.

Row 6: K2, yo, {k5}, yo, k2, yo, {k5 (5, 5, 5, 7), yo, k3tog, yo, k5 (5, 5, 5, 7)}, yo, k2, yo, {k5, [yo, k3tog, yo, k3] 3 (4, 5, 6, 7) times, yo, k3tog, yo, k5}, yo, k2, yo, {k5 (5, 5, 5, 7), yo, k3tog, yo, k5 (5, 5, 5, 7)}, yo, k2, yo, {k5}, yo, k2—89 (95, 97, 101, 121) sts.

Row 8: K2, yo, {k7}, yo, k2, yo, {k3 (3, 3, 3, 5), yo, k3tog, yo, [k3, yo, k3tog, yo] 1 time, k3 (3, 3, 3, 5)}, yo, k2, yo, {[k3, yo, k3tog, yo] 5 (6, 7, 8, 9) times, k3}, yo, k2, yo, {k3 (3, 3, 3, 5), yo k3tog, yo, [k3, yo, k3tog, yo] 1 time, k3 (3, 3, 3, 5)}, yo, k2, yo, {k7}, yo, k2—99 (105, 107, 111, 131) sts.

Row 10: K2, yo, {k3, yo, k3tog, yo, k3}, yo, k2, yo, {k1 (1, 1, 1, 3), [yo, k3tog, yo, k3] 2 times, yo, k3tog, yo, k1 (1, 1, 1, 3)}, yo, k2, yo, {k1, [yo, k3tog, yo, k3] 5 (6, 7, 8, 9) times, yo, k3tog, yo, k1}, yo, k2, yo, {k1 (1, 1, 1, 3), [yo, k3tog, yo, k3] 2 times, yo, k3tog, yo, k1 (1, 1, 1, 3)}, yo, k2, yo, {k3, yo, k3tog, yo, k3}, yo, k2—109 (115, 117, 121, 141) sts.

Row 12: K2, yo, {k1, yo, k3tog, yo, k3, yo, k3tog, yo, k1}, yo, k2, yo, {k5 (5, 5, 5, 7), yo, k3tog, yo, k3, yo, k3tog, yo, k5 (5, 5, 5, 7)}, yo, k2, yo, {k5, [yo, k3tog, yo, k3] 4 (5, 6, 7, 8) times, yo, k3tog, yo, k5}, yo, k2, yo, {k5 (5, 5, 5, 7), yo, k3tog, yo, k3, yo, k3tog, yo, k5 (5, 5, 5, 7)}, yo, k2, yo, {k1, yo, k3tog, yo, k3, yo, k3tog, yo, k1}, yo, k2—119 (125, 127, 131, 151) sts.

Row 14: K2, yo, {k5, yo, k3tog, yo, k5}, yo, k2, yo, {k3 (3, 3, 3, 5), yo, k3tog, yo, [k3, yo, k3tog, yo] 2 times, k3 (3, 3, 3, 5)}, yo, k2, yo, {[k3, yo, k3tog, yo] 6 (7, 8, 9, 10) times, k3}, yo, k2, yo, {k3 (3, 3, 3, 5), yo, k3tog, yo, [k3, yo, k3tog, yo] 2 times, k3 (3, 3, 3, 5)}, yo, k2, yo, {k5, yo, k3tog, yo, k5}, yo, k2—129 (135, 137, 141, 161) sts.

Row 16: K2, yo, {[k3, yo, k3tog, yo] 2 times, k3}, yo, k2, yo, {k1 (1, 1, 1, 3), [yo, k3tog, yo, k3] 3 times, yo, k3tog, yo, k1 (1, 1, 1, 3)}, yo, k2, yo, {k1, [yo, k3tog, yo, k3] 6 (7, 8, 9, 10) times, yo, k3tog, yo, k1}, yo, k2, yo, {k1 (1, 1, 1, 3), [yo, k3tog, yo, k3] 3 times, yo, k3tog, yo, k1 (1, 1, 1, 3)}, yo, k2, yo, {[k3, yo, k3tog, yo] 2 times, k3}, yo, k2—139 (145, 147. 151, 171) sts.

Row 18: K2, {k1, [yo, k3tog, yo, k3] 2 times, yo, k3tog, yo, k1}, yo, k2, yo, {k5 (5, 5, 5, 7), [yo, k3tog, yo, k3] 2 times, yo, k3tog, yo, k5 (5, 5, 5, 7)}, yo, k2, yo, {k5, [yo, k3tog, yo, k3] 5 (6, 7, 8, 9) times, yo, k3tog, yo, k5}, yo, k2, yo, {k5 (5, 5, 5,

7), [yo, k3tog, yo, k3] 2 times, yo, k3tog, yo, k5 (5, 5, 5, 7)}, yo, k2, yo, {k1, [yo, k3tog, yo, k3] 2 times, yo, k3tog, yo, k1}, k2—147 (153, 155, 159, 179) sts.

Row 20: K2, {k4, {yo, k3tog, yo, k3, yo, k3tog, yo, k4}, yo, k2, yo, {k3 (3, 3, 3, 5), [yo, k3tog, yo, k3] 3 times}, yo, k3tog, yo, k3 (3, 3, 3, 5)}, yo, k2, yo, {k3, [yo, k3tog, yo, k3] 7 (8, 9, 10, 11) times}, yo, k2, yo, {k3 (3, 3, 3, 5), [yo, k3tog, yo, k3] 3 times, yo, k3tog, yo, k3 (3, 3, 3, 5)}, yo, k2, yo, {k5, {yo, k3tog, yo, k3, yo, k3tog, yo, k4}, k2—155 (161, 163, 167, 187) sts.

Row 22: K2, {k1, [yo, k3tog, yo, k3] 3 times}, yo, k2, yo, {k1 (1, 1, 1, 3), [yo, k3tog, yo, k3] 4 times, yo, k3tog, yo, k1

(1, 1, 1, 3)}, yo, k2, yo, {k1, [yo, k3tog, yo, k3] 7 (8, 9, 10, 11) times, yo, k3tog, yo, k1}, yo, k2, yo, {k1 (1, 1, 1, 3), [yo, k3tog, yo, k3] 4 times, yo, k3tog, yo, k1 (1, 1, 1, 3)}, yo, k2, yo, {[k3, yo, k3tog, yo] 3 times, k1}, yo, k2—163 (169, 171, 175, 195) sts.

Row 24: K2, {k4, [yo, k3tog, yo, k3] 2 times, yo, k3tog, yo, k1}, yo, k2, yo, {k5 (5, 5, 5, 7), [yo, k3tog, yo, k3] 3 times, yo, k3tog, yo, k5 (5, 5, 5, 7)}, yo, k2, yo, {k5, [yo, k3tog, yo, k3] 6 (7, 8, 9, 10) times, yo, k3tog, yo, k5}, yo, k2, yo, {k5 (5, 5, 5, 7), [yo, k3tog, yo, k3] 3 times, yo, k3tog, yo, k5 (5, 5, 5, 7)}, yo, k2, yo, {k1, [yo, k3tog, yo, k3] 2 times, yo, k3tog, k4}, k2—171 (177, 179, 183, 203) sts.

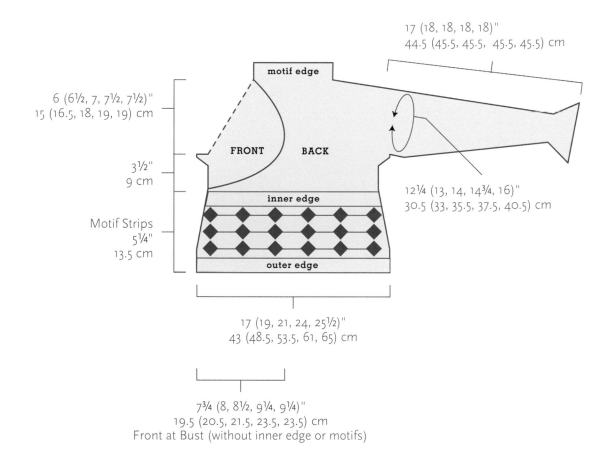

17 (18, 18, 18, 18)"
44.5 (45.5, 45.5, 45.5, 45.5) cm

motif edge

6 (6½, 7, 7½, 7½)"
15 (16.5, 18, 19, 19) cm

FRONT   BACK

3½"
9 cm

inner edge

12¼ (13, 14, 14¾, 16)"
30.5 (33, 35.5, 37.5, 40.5) cm

Motif Strips
5¼"
13.5 cm

outer edge

17 (19, 21, 24, 25½)"
43 (48.5, 53.5, 61, 65) cm

7¾ (8, 8½, 9¼, 9¼)"
19.5 (20.5, 21.5, 23.5, 23.5) cm
Front at Bust (without inner edge or motifs)

Row 26: K2, {k1, [yo, k3tog, yo, k3] 2 times, yo, k3tog, yo, k5}, yo, k2, yo, {k3 (3, 3, 3, 5), [yo, k3tog, yo, k3] 4 times, yo, k3tog, yo, k3 (3, 3, 3, 5)}, yo, k2, yo, {k3, [yo, k3tog, yo, k3] 8 (9, 10, 11, 12) times}, yo, k2, yo, {k3 (3, 3, 3, 5), [yo, k3tog, yo, k3] 4 times, yo, k3tog, yo, k3 (3, 3, 3, 5)}, yo, k2, yo, {k5, [yo, k3tog, yo, k3] 2 times, yo, k3tog, yo, k1}, k2—179 (185, 187, 191, 211) sts.

Row 28: K2, {k4, [yo, k3tog, yo, k3] 3 times}, yo, k2, yo, {k1 (1, 1, 1, 3), [yo, k3tog, yo, k3] 5 times, yo, k3tog, yo, k1 (1, 1, 1, 3)}, yo, k2, yo, {k1, [yo, k3tog, yo, k3] 8 (9, 10, 11, 12) times, yo, k3tog, yo, k1}, yo, k2, yo, {k1 (1, 1, 1, 3), [yo, k3tog, yo, k3] 5 times, yo, k3tog, yo, k1 (1, 1, 1, 3)}, yo, k2, yo, {[k3, yo, k3tog, yo] 3 times, k4}, k2—187 (193, 195, 199, 219) sts.

Row 30: K2, {k1, [yo, k3tog, yo, k3] 3 times, yo, k3tog, yo, k1}, yo, k2, yo, {k5 (5, 5, 5, 7), [yo, k3tog, yo, k3] 4 times, yo, k3tog, yo, k5 (5, 5, 5, 7)}, yo, k2, yo, {k5, [yo, k3tog, yo, k3] 7 (8, 9, 10, 11) times, yo, k3tog, yo, k5}, yo, k2, yo, {k5 (5, 5, 5, 7), [yo, k3tog, yo, k3] 4 times, yo, k3tog, yo, k5 (5, 5, 5, 7)}, yo, k2, yo, {k1, [yo, k3tog, yo, k3] 3 times, yo, k3tog, yo, k1}, k2—195 (201, 203, 207, 227) sts.

FOR SIZES 35 (38, 42½, 44)" ONLY

Row 32: K2, {k4, [yo k3tog, yo, k3] 3 times, k2}, yo, k2, yo, {k3 (3, 3, 5). [Yo, k3tog, yo, k3] 5 times, yo, k3tog, yo, k3 (3, 3, 5)}, yo, k2, yo, {k3, [yo, k3tog, yo, k3] 9 (10, 11, 12) times}, yo, k2, yo, {k3 (3, 3, 5). [Yo, k3tog, yo, k3] 5 times, yo, k3tog, yo, k3 (3, 3, 5)}, yo, k2, yo, {k2, [yo, k3tog, yo, k3] 3 times, k4}, k2—209 (211, 215, 235) sts.

FOR SIZES 38 (42½, 44)" ONLY

Row 34: K2, {k1, [yo, k3tog, yo, k3] 4 times}, yo, k2, yo {k1 (1, 3), [yo, k3tog, yo, k3] 6 times, yo, k3tog, yo, k1 (1, 3)}, yo, k2, yo, {k1, [yo, k3tog, yo, k3] 11 (12, 13) times, yo, k3tog, yo, k1}, yo, k2, yo, {k1 (1, 3), [yo, k3tog, yo, k3] 6 times, yo, k3tog, yo, k1 (1, 3)}, yo, k2, yo, {k1, [yo, k3tog, yo, k3] 11 (12, 13) times, yo, k3tog, yo, k1}, yo, k2, yo, {[k3, yo, k3tog, yo] 4 times}, k2—219 (223, 243) sts.

Row 36: K2, {k5, [yo, k3tog, yo, k3] 3 times, yo, k3tog, yo, k1}, yo, k2, yo, {k5 (5, 7), [yo, k3tog, yo, k3] 5 times, yo, k3tog, yo, k5 (5, 7)}, yo, k2, yo, {k5, [yo, k3tog, yo, k3] 10 (11, 12) times, yo, k3tog, yo, k5}, yo, k2, yo, {k5 (5, 7), [yo, k3tog, yo, k3] 5 times, yo, k3tog, yo, k5 (5, 7)}, yo, k2, yo, {k1, [yo, k3tog, yo, k3] 3 times, yo, k3tog, yo, k2}, k2—227 (231, 251) sts.

FOR SIZES 42½ (44)" ONLY

Row 38: K2, {k1, [yo, k3tog, yo, k3] 3 times, yo, k3tog, yo, k5}, yo, k2, yo, {k3 (5), [yo, k3tog, yo, k3] 6 times, yo, k3tog, yo, k3 (5)}, yo, k2, yo, {k3, [yo, k3tog, yo, k3] 13 (14) times}, yo, k2, yo, {k3 (5), [yo, k3tog, yo, k3] 6 times, yo, k3tog, yo, k3 (5)}, yo, k2, yo, {k5, [yo, k3tog, yo, k3] 3 times, yo, k3tog, yo, k1}, k2—239 (239, 259) sts.

FOR ALL SIZES

Knit across right front 27 (28, 30, 32, 32) sts, slip right sleeve 41 (43, 47, 47, 49) sts to a holder, CO 8 (8, 8, 10, 10) sts using knitted CO (see Glossary), knit across back

59 (67, 77, 85, 91) sts, slip left sleeve 41 (43, 47, 47, 49) sts to a holder, CO 8 (8, 8, 10, 10) sts using knitted CO, knit across left front 27 (28, 30, 32, 32) sts—129 (139, 153, 169, 175) sts.

Knit 5 more rows.

Lace Lower Body Pattern

NOTE: *Lace pattern is multiple of 6 + 3.*

Row 1: K3 (5, 3, 5, 5), [yo, k3tog, yo, k3] 20 (21, 24, 26, 27) times, yo, k3tog, yo, k3 (5, 3, 5, 5)—129 (139, 153, 169, 175) sts.

Row 2: Knit.

Row 3: K3 (5, 3, 5, 5), [k3, yo, k3tog, yo] 20 (21, 24, 26, 27) times, k6 (8, 6, 8, 8).

Row 4: Knit.

Rep rows 1–4 for 4" (10 cm).

Dec at lower front edges as follows:

Next row: K3 (5, 3, 5, 5), k3tog, k3, [yo, k3tog, yo, k3] 19 (20, 23, 25, 26) times, k3tog, k3 (5, 3, 5, 5)—125 (135, 149, 165, 171) sts.

Next row: Knit.

Next row: K3 (5, 3, 5, 5), k3tog, k1, [k3, yo, k3tog, yo] 19 (20, 23, 25, 26) times, k3tog, k1 (3, 1, 3, 3)—121 (131, 145, 161, 167) sts.

Next row: Knit.

Next row: K3 (5, 3, 5, 5), k3tog, k2tog, yo, [k3, yo, k3tog, yo] 18 (19, 22, 24, 25) times, k3tog, k2 (4, 2, 4, 4)—117 (127, 141, 157, 163) sts.

Next 6 rows: Knit.

BO loosely.

Motif Edging

With dpn, CO 3 sts; do not join.

Row 1: (RS) K1f&b, yo, k2—5 sts.

Rows 2, 4, 6, 8, 10: (WS) Knit across.

Row 3: K2, yo, k1, yo, k2—7 sts.

Row 5: K2, yo, k3, yo, k2—9 sts.

Row 7: K1, ssk, yo, s2kp, yo, k2tog, k1—7 sts.

Row 9: K1, ssk, yo, k3tog, k1—5 sts.

Row 11: Ssk, k1, k2tog—3 sts.

Row 12: S2kp—1 st.

Row 13: Knit into the front, back, and front of the same st—3 sts.

Row 14: Rep Row 2.

FIRST STRIP

Rep Rows 1–14 until you have 30 (32, 34, 37, 39) medallions, end last motif at Row 12. Sew final 3 sts to the 3 sts beginning the first motif. Fasten off.

SECOND STRIP

*Rep Rows 1–5 of first medallion, pick up and knit along edge of adjacent medallion on first strip. For Row 6, knit picked-up st and first st tog, knit across—9 sts. Rep Rows 7–14 of first medallion. Rep from * until you have 30 (32, 34, 37, 39) medallions in this strip, but end last medallion at Row 12. Sew final 3 sts to the 3 sts beginning the first motif. Fasten off.

THIRD STRIP

*Rep Rows 1–5 of first medallion, pick up and knit along edge of adjacent medallion on second strip. For Row 6, knit picked-up st and first st tog, knit across—9 sts. Rep Rows 7–14 of first medallion. Rep from * until you have 30 (32, 34, 37, 39) medallions in this strip, but end last motif at Row 12. Sew final 3 sts to the 3 sts beginning the first motif. Fasten off.

Block medallion fabric before continuing.

INNER EDGE SIDE OF FABRIC (TO BE JOINED TO BODY OF SWEATER)

NOTE: *One long side of the motifs will be worked evenly and one side will be gathered so the fabric has a curve to it and will ease into the body of the sweater nicely. You will pick up and knit into the side of a medallion, then knit CO sts between the medallions before picking up and knitting into the next medallion. On the decrease/gather side, you will pick up and knit into 2 medallions at once (double thickness of fabric).*

Row 1: (Pick up and knit into the side center of the first medallion) 2 times, CO 8 sts using knitted CO. *(Pick up and knit into the side center of the next medallion) 2 times, CO 8 sts using knitted CO. Rep from * 7 (10, 11, 11, 11) more times. On next repeat, **pick up and knit into the next 2 medallions simultaneously (as a double thickness). CO 8 sts***. Rep from * 2 (2, 2, 3, 3) more times regular. Rep from ** to *** 3 (4, 4, 5, 5) times through double thickness of 2 medallions held together on each repeat. Rep from * 2 (2, 2, 3, 3) times regular. Rep from ** to *** once more through double thickness of 2 medallions held together. Rep from * 7 (10, 11, 11, 11) more times regular, then (pick up and knit into the side center of the final medallion) 2 times.

Row 2: Knit.

Rows 3–10: Knit.

BO all sts loosely.

OUTER EDGE SIDE OF FABRIC (NOT JOINED TO BODY OF SWEATER)

Row 1: (Pick up and knit into the side center of the first medallion) 2 times, CO 8 sts using knitted CO, *(pick up and knit into the side center of the next medallion) 2 times, CO 8 sts using knitted CO. Rep from * across—300 (320, 340, 370, 390) sts.

Rows 2–10: Knit.

FOR SIZES 32½ (44)" ONLY

*CO 3 sts using knitted CO, BO 6 sts. Rep from * around to last 2 sts. CO 3 sts using knitted CO, BO 5 sts.

FOR SIZE 35" ONLY

*CO 3 sts using knitted CO, BO 6 sts. Rep from * around to last 2 sts. CO 3 sts using knitted CO, BO 5 sts.

FOR SIZES 38 (42½)" ONLY

*CO 3 sts using knitted CO, BO 6 sts. Rep from * around to last 4 sts. CO 3 sts using knitted CO, BO 7 sts.

Sleeves

Move 41 (43, 47, 47, 49) sts from sleeve holder to needles.

Row 1: Attach yarn and knit across.

Row 2: Knit to end, then pick up and knit 4 (4, 4, 5, 5) sts from half of the body underarm sts.

Row 3: Knit to end, then pick up and knit 4 (4, 4, 5, 5) sts from other half of the body underarm sts—49 (51, 55, 57, 59) sts.

Continue knitting in garter st until sleeve measures 17 (18, 18, 18, 18)" (44.5 [45.5, 45.5, 45.5, 45.5] cm).

FOR SIZES 32½ (38)" ONLY

*CO 3 sts using knitted CO, BO 6 sts. Rep from * to last 4 sts. CO 3 sts using knitted CO, BO 7 sts.

FOR SIZES 35 (42½)" ONLY

*CO 3 sts using knitted CO, BO 6 sts. Rep from * across.

FOR SIZE 44" ONLY

*CO 3 sts using knitted CO, BO 6 sts. Rep from * to last 2 sts. CO 3 sts using knitted CO, BO 5 sts.

Finishing

Sew sleeve seams. Weave in all ends. Block to measurements.

ABBREVIATIONS

4/4LC	slide 4 sts to cn and hold in front of work, k2, k2 from cn
4/4RC	slide 4 sts to cn and hold in back of work, k2, k2 from cn
beg(s)	begin(s); beginning
BO	bind off
C4B	slide 2 sts to cn and hold to the back of the work, k2, k2 from cn
C4F	slide 2 sts to cn and hold to the front of the work, k2, k2 from cn
cir	circular
cm	centimeter(s)
cn	cable needle
CO	cast on
cont	continue(s); continuing
dec(s)('d)	decrease(s); decreasing; decreased
dpn	double-pointed needles
foll(s)	follow(s); following
g	gram(s)
inc(s)('d)	increase(s); increasing; increased
k	knit
k1f&b	knit into the front and back of same stitch
k2tog	knit 2 stitches together
k3tog	knit 3 stitches together
kfbf	knit into the front, back, and the front again of same stitch
kwise	knitwise, as if to knit
m	marker(s)
mm	millimeter(s)
M1	make one (increase)
M1L	make one (increase) with a left slant
M1R	make one (increase) with a right slant
oz	ounce
p	purl
p1f&b	purl into front and back of same stitch
p2sso	pass 2 stitches over last stitch

p2tog	purl 2 stitches together
p3sso:	pass 3 stitches over last stitch
patt(s)	pattern(s)
pm	place marker
psso	pass slipped stitch over
pwise	purlwise; as if to purl
rem	remain(s); remaining
rep	repeat(s); repeating
Rev St st	reverse stockinette stitch
rnd(s)	round(s)
RS	right side
s2kp	slip 2 stitches knitwise, one at a time, knit the next stitch, pass slipped stitches over knit stitch
s2k2p	slip 2 stitches knitwise, one at a time, knit 2 stitches together, pass slipped stitches over k2tog
s3k2p	slip 3 stitches knitwise, one at a time, knit 2 stitches together, pass slipped stitches over k2tog
sl	slip
sl st	slip stitch (slip stitch purlwise unless otherwise indicated)
ssk	slip 2 stitches knitwise, one at a time, from the left needle to right needle, insert left needle tip through both front loops and knit together from this position
st(s)	stitch(es)
St st	stockinette stitch
tbl	through back loop
tog	together
WS	wrong side
wyb	with yarn in back
wyf	with yarn in front
yd	yard(s)
yo	yarnover
*	repeat starting point
* *	repeat all instructions between asterisks
( )	alternate measurements and/or instructions
[ ]	work instructions as a group a specified number of times

GLOSSARY

Bind-Offs

Chain-2 Bind-Off

*Bind off one stitch (**Figure 1**), [yarn over (**Figure 2**), pull the first stitch over the yarnover as if to bind off] three times (or number of times called for in pattern) to form a chain (**Figure 3**)—one stitch bound off; repeat from * for desired number of stitches.

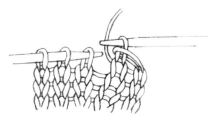

Figure 1

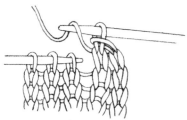

Figure 2

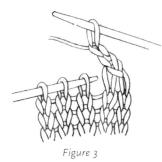

Figure 3

Standard Bind-Off

Knit the first stitch, *knit the next stitch (two stitches on right needle), insert left needle tip into first stitch on right needle (**Figure 1**) and lift this stitch up and over the second stitch (**Figure 2**) and off the needle (**Figure 3**). Repeat from * for the desired number of stitches.

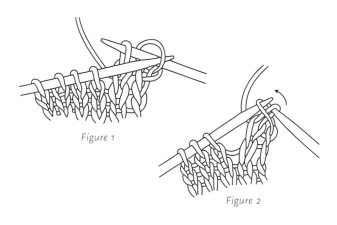

Figure 1

Figure 2

Figure 3

Three-Needle Bind-Off

Place the stitches to be joined onto two separate needles and hold the needles parallel so that the right sides of knitting face together. Insert a third needle into the first stitch on each of two needles (**Figure 1**) and knit them together as one stitch (**Figure 2**), *knit the next stitch on each needle the same way, then use the left needle tip to lift the first stitch over the second and off the needle (**Figure 3**). Repeat from * until no stitches remain on first two needles. Cut yarn and pull tail through last stitch to secure.

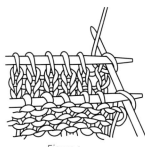

Figure 1

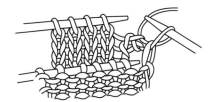

Figure 2

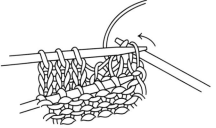

Figure 3

Yarn-Over Bind-Off

Knit one stitch, *yarn over, knit one stitch (**Figure 1**), then lift the yarnover and the first stitch over the second stitch and off the needle (**Figure 2**) to bind off one stitch; repeat from * for desired number of stitches.

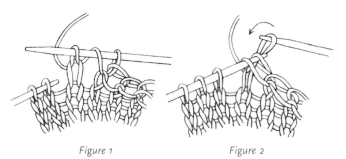

Figure 1   *Figure 2*

Blocking
Mist Blocking

Generously spray both right and wrong sides with water mixed with a few drops of no-rinse wash for delicate fibers. Lay on a flat surface, pin to desired dimensions, if necessary, and let dry completely before moving.

Steam Blocking

Pin the pieces to be blocked to a blocking surface. Hold an iron set on the steam setting ½" (1.3 cm) above the knitted surface and direct the steam over the entire surface (except ribbing). You can get similar results by lapping wet cheesecloth on top of the knitted surface and touching it lightly with a dry iron. Lift and set down the iron gently; do not use a pushing motion. This is not the most accurate method of blocking, but it will give you quick results that dry quickly.

Wet-Towel Blocking

This is usually the most accurate method for swatching and achieving your final gauge. Add a teaspoon of no-rinse delicate wash to a sink or large bowl full of lukewarm water and submerge your swatch or project. Let it soak and absorb the water for 10–15 minutes. Press out the excess water with fresh towels (do not ring or twist fabric as it may cause damage). Lay flat to dry, and pin to finished measurements if applicable.

Care

In order to preserve your handknitted garments for a lifetime of wear, be sure to store and clean them properly. Fold your garments and place them on shelves rather than hanging them, as this may stretch them. Avoid using harsh dry cleaning chemicals and detergents. Wash with an all-natural wash for delicates to remove oils and condition and preserve the fibers of the yarn.

Cast-Ons
Backward-Loop Cast-On

*Loop working yarn and place it on needle backward so that it doesn't unwind. Repeat from *.

Cable Cast-On

If there are no stitches on the needles, make a slipknot of working yarn and place it on the left needle, then use the knitted method to cast on one more stitch—two stitches on needle. When there are at least two stitches on the left needle, hold needle with working yarn in your left hand. *Insert right needle between the first two stitches on left needle (**Figure 1**), wrap yarn around needle as if to knit, draw yarn through (**Figure 2**), and place new loop on left needle (**Figure 3**) to form a new stitch. Repeat from * for the desired number of stitches, always working between the first two stitches on the left needle.

Figure 1

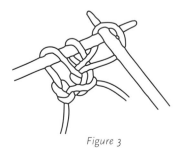

Figure 2

Figure 3

Knitted Cast-On

If there are no stitches on the needles, make a slipknot of working yarn and place it on the left needle. When there is at least one stitch on the left needle, *use the right needle to knit the first stitch (or slipknot) on left needle (**Figure 1**) and place new loop onto left needle to form a new stitch (**Figure 2**). Repeat from * for the desired number of stitches, always working into the last stitch made.

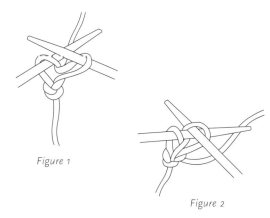

Figure 1

Figure 2

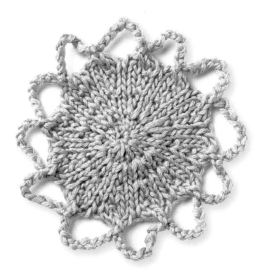

Long-Tail (Continental) Cast-On

Leaving a long tail (about ½" [1.3 cm] for each stitch to be cast on), make a slipknot and place on right needle. Place thumb and index finger of your left hand between the yarn ends so that working yarn is around your index finger and tail end is around your thumb and secure the yarn ends with your other fingers. Hold your palm upward, making a V of yarn (**Figure 1**). *Bring needle up through loop on thumb (**Figure 2**), catch first strand around index finger, and go back down through loop on thumb (**Figure 3**). Drop loop off thumb and, placing thumb back in V configuration, tighten resulting stitch on needle (**Figure 4**). Repeat from * for the desired number of stitches.

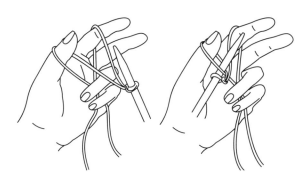

Figure 1

Figure 2

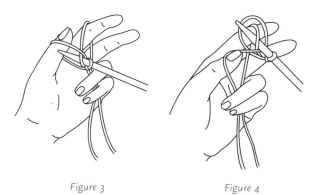

Figure 3

Figure 4

Möbius Cast-On

This technique and the accompanying illustrations come from Jeny Staiman of curiousknitter.blogspot.com. Starting with a long circular needle (40" [101.5 cm] works fine), tie a slipknot and place it on your right-hand needle. Loop the cable around, and place it in front of the knotted working yarn, holding the yarn behind the needle and cable (**Figure 1**). With your left (working hand) in front of the cable, pull the ball of yarn through the cabled loop and bring up and over the needle and back behind the needle. The yarn is wrapped around the needle and the cable (this is the first Möbius stitch). When counting stitches, count this wrap as one stitch. Continue to wrap the yarn through the cable, up and over the needle and back behind it for your specified stitch count, sliding the accumulated stitches off the right needle and onto the cables (**Figure 2**). Keep your tension loose as you slide the stitches onto the cable. When your stitches wrap around your cable and onto the left-hand needle, you are ready to begin knitting. Place a stitch marker on the right-hand needle to mark the beginning and end of your rounds (**Figure 3**). **NOTE:** *One revolution in a Möbius is actually a figure eight, or a top round and bottom round of your twisted tube.*

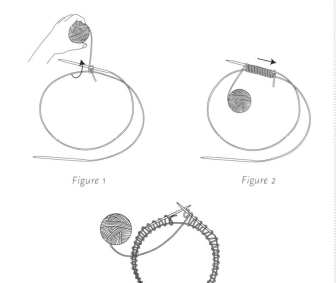

Figure 1   Figure 2

Figure 3

Crochet
Crochet Chain (ch)

Make a slipknot and place it on crochet hook if there isn't a loop already on the hook. *Yarn over hook and draw through loop on hook. Repeat from * for the desired number of stitches. To fasten off, cut yarn and draw end through last loop formed.

Single Crochet (sc)

*Insert hook into the second chain from the hook (or the next stitch), yarn over hook and draw through a loop, yarn over hook (**Figure 1**), and draw it through both loops on hook (**Figure 2**). Repeat from * for the desired number of stitches.

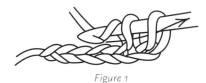

Figure 1

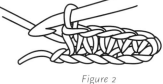

Figure 2

Decreases

Knit 2 Together (k2tog)
Knit two stitches together as if they were a single stitch.

Knit 3 Together (k3tog)
Knit three stitches together as if they were a single stitch.

Purl 2 Together (p2tog)
Purl two stitches together as if they were a single stitch.

Purl 3 Together (p3tog)
Purl three stitches together as if they were a single stitch.

Slip, Slip, Knit (ssk)
Slip two stitches individually knitwise (**Figure 1**), insert left needle tip into the front of these two slipped stitches, and use the right needle to knit them together through their back loops (**Figure 2**).

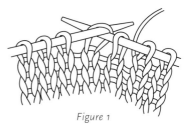

Figure 1

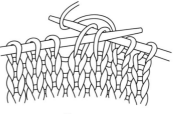

Figure 2

Slip, Slip, Slip, Knit (sssk)
Slip three stitches individually knitwise, insert left needle tip into the front of these three slipped stitches, and use the right needle to knit them together through their back loops.

Slip, Slip, Purl (ssp)
Holding yarn in front, slip two stitches individually knitwise (**Figure 1**), then slip these two stitches back onto left needle (they will be twisted on the needle), and purl them together through their back loops (**Figure 2**).

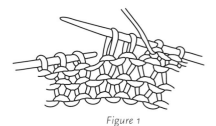

Figure 1

Figure 2

Gauge

Knit a swatch at least 4" (10 cm) square. Remove the stitches from the needles or bind them off loosely and lay the swatch on a flat surface. Place a ruler over the swatch and count the number of stitches across and number of rows down (including fractions of stitches and rows) in 4" (10 cm) and divide this number by four to get the number of stitches (including fractions of stitches) in one inch. Repeat two or three times on different areas of the swatch to confirm the measurements. If you have more stitches and rows than called for in the instructions, knit another swatch with larger needles; if you have fewer stitches and rows, knit another swatch with smaller needles. If you will be blocking your finished garment, block your swatch to achieve the most accurate gauge.

I-Cord (also called Knit-Cord)

This is worked with two double pointed needles. Cast on the desired number of stitches (usually three to four). Knit across these stitches, then *without turning the needle, slide stitches to other end of needle, pull the yarn around the back, and knit the stitches as usual. Repeat from * for desired length.

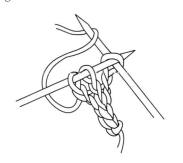

Increases
Bar Increase
KNITWISE (K1F&B)

Knit into a stitch but leave the stitch on the left needle (**Figure 1**), then knit through the back loop of the same stitch (**Figure 2**) and slip the original stitch off the needle (**Figure 3**).

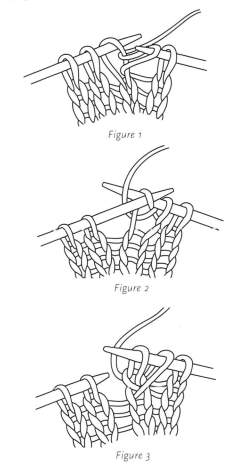

Figure 1

Figure 2

Figure 3

PURLWISE (P1F&B)

Work as for a knitwise bar increase, but purl into the front and back of the same stitch.

Raised Make-One (M1) Increase

NOTE: *Use the left slant if no direction of slant is specified.*

LEFT SLANT (M1L)

With left needle tip, lift the strand between the last knitted stitch and the first stitch on the left needle from front to back (**Figure 1**), then knit the lifted loop through the back (**Figure 2**).

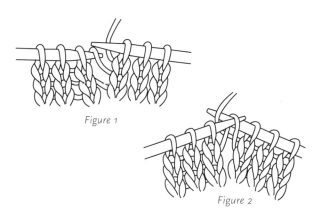

Figure 1

Figure 2

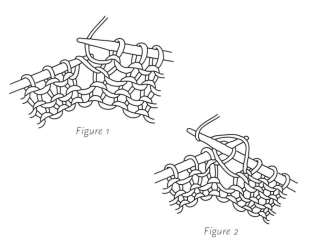

RIGHT SLANT (M1R)

With left needle tip, lift the strand between the needles from back to front (**Figure 1**). Knit the lifted loop through the front (**Figure 2**).

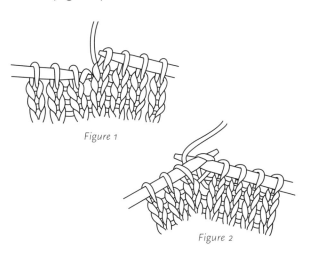

Figure 1

Figure 2

PURLWISE (M1P)

With left needle tip, lift the strand between the needles from front to back (**Figure 1**), then purl the lifted loop through the back (**Figure 2**).

Figure 1

Figure 2

Joining for Working in Rounds

For projects that begin with ribbing or stockinette st, simply arrange the stitches for working in rounds, then knit the first stitch that was cast on to form a tube.

For projects that begin with seed, garter, or reverse stockinette st, arrange the needle so that the yarn tail is at the left needle tip. Holding the yarn in back, slip the first st from the right needle onto the left needle (**Figure 1**), bring the yarn to the front between the two needles, and slip the first two stitches from the left tip to the right tip (**Figure 2**), then bring the yarn to the back between the two needles and slip the first stitch from the right tip to the left tip (**Figure 3**).

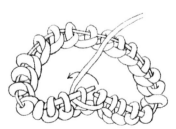

Figure 1

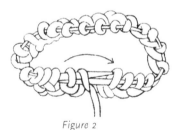

Figure 2

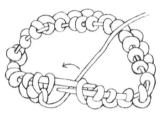

Figure 3

Pick Up and Knit
Along CO or BO Edge

With right side facing and working from right to left, insert the tip of the needle into the center of the stitch below the bind-off or cast-on edge (**Figure 1**), wrap yarn around needle, and pull through a loop (**Figure 2**). Pick up one stitch for every existing stitch.

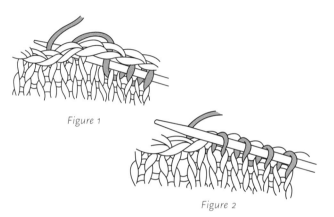

Figure 1

Figure 2

Along Shaped Edge

With right side facing and working from right to left, insert tip of needle between last and second-to-last stitches, wrap yarn around needle, and pull through a loop. Pick up and knit about three stitches for every four rows, adjusting as necessary so that picked-up edge lays flat.

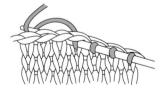

Seams

Backstitch Seam—Horizontal

Pin pieces to be seamed with right sides facing together. Working from right to left into the stitch just below the bind-off row, bring threaded needle up between the second two stitches on each piece of knitted fabric, then back down through both layers, one stitch to the right of the starting point (**Figure 1**). *Bring the needle up through both layers one stitch to the left of the backstitch just made (**Figure 2**), then back down to the right, through the same hole used before (**Figure 3**). Repeat from *, working backward one stitch for every two stitches worked forward.

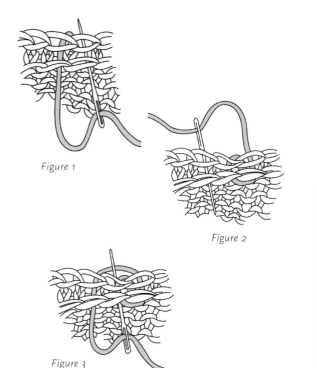

Figure 1

Figure 2

Figure 3

Grafting

HORIZONTAL GRAFTING

Working with the bound-off edges opposite each other, right sides of the knitting facing you, and working into the stitches just below the bound-off edges, bring threaded tapestry needle out at the center of the first stitch (i.e., go under half of the first stitch) on one side of the seam, then bring needle in and out under the first whole stitch on the other side (**Figure 1**). *Bring needle into the center of the same stitch it came out of before, then out in the center of the adjacent stitch (**Figure 2**). Bring needle in and out under the next whole stitch on the other side (**Figure 3**). Repeat from *, ending with a half-stitch on the first side.

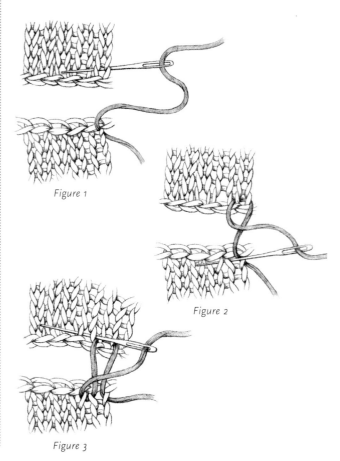

Figure 1

Figure 2

Figure 3

KITCHENER STITCH

Arrange stitches on two needles so that there is an equal number of stitches on each needle. Hold the needles parallel to each other with wrong sides of the knitting together. Allowing about ½" (1.3 cm) per stitch to be grafted, thread matching yarn on a tapestry needle. Work from right to left as follows:

Step 1. Bring tapestry needle through the first stitch on the front needle as if to purl and leave the stitch on the needle (**Figure 1**).

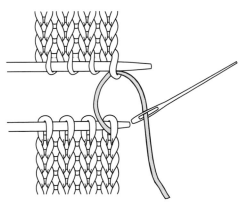

Figure 1

Step 2. Bring tapestry needle through the fi rst stitch on the back needle as if to knit and leave that stitch on the needle (**Figure 2**).

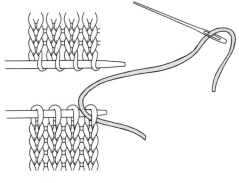

Figure 2

Step 3. Bring tapestry needle through the first front stitch as if to knit and slip this stitch off the needle. Then bring tapestry needle through the next front stitch as if to purl and leave this stitch on the needle (**Figure 3**).

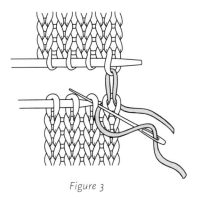

Figure 3

Step 4. Bring tapestry needle through the first back stitch as if to purl and slip this stitch off the needle. Then bring tapestry needle through the next back stitch as if to knit and leave this stitch on the needle (**Figure 4**).

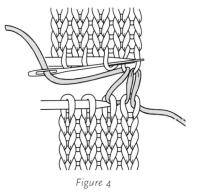

Figure 4

Repeat Steps 3 and 4 until one stitch remains on each needle, adjusting the tension to match the rest of the knitting as you go. To finish, bring tapestry needle through the front stitch as if to knit and slip this stitch off the needle. Then bring tapestry needle through the back stitch as if to purl and slip this stitch off the needle.

Mattress Stitch

Place the pieces to be seamed on a table, right sides facing up. Begin at the lower edge and work upward as follows for your stitch pattern:

STOCKINETTE STITCH WITH 1-STITCH SEAM ALLOWANCE

Insert threaded needle under one bar between the two edge stitches on one piece, then under the corresponding bar plus the bar above it on the other piece (**Figure 1**). *Pick up the next two bars on the first piece (**Figure 2**), then the next two bars on the other (**Figure 3**). Repeat from *, ending by picking up the last bar or pair of bars on the first piece.

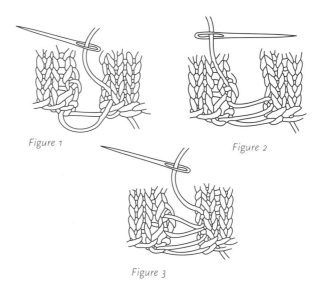

Figure 1

Figure 2

Figure 3

VERTICAL-TO-HORIZONTAL GRAFTING

*Bring threaded tapestry needle from back to front in the V of a knit stitch just below the bound-off edge. Insert the needle under one or two bars between the first and second stitch in from the selvedge edge on the adjacent piece, then back to the front of the same knit stitch just under the bound-off edge. Repeat from *, striving to match the tension of the knitting.

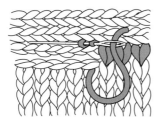

STOCKINETTE STITCH WITH ½-STITCH SEAM ALLOWANCE

To reduce bulk in the mattress stitch seam, work as for the 1-stitch seam allowance but pick up the bars in the center of the edge stitches instead of between the last two stitches.

Slip-Stitch Crochet

To begin, place a slipknot on a crochet hook. With wrong sides facing together and working one stitch at a time, *insert crochet hook through both thicknesses into the edge stitches (**Figure 1**), grab a loop of yarn and draw this loop through both thicknesses, then through the loop on the hook (**Figure 2**).

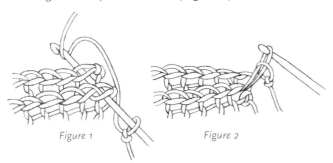

Figure 1   Figure 2

Whipstitch

Hold pieces to be sewn together so that the edges to be seamed are even with each other. With yarn threaded on a tapestry needle, *insert needle through both layers from back to front, then bring needle to back in a spiral. Repeat from *, keeping even tension on the seaming yarn.

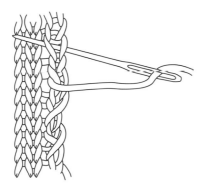

Wrap-3

Bring yarn to the front, slip three stitches purlwise (**Figure 1**), bring the yarn to the back, slip the same three stitches back onto the left-hand needle (**Figure 2**), then knit the same three stitches.

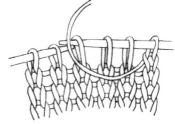

Figure 1

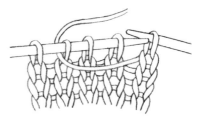

Figure 2

RESOURCES

Alpaca Yarn Company
144 Roosevelt Ave., Bay #1
York, PA 17401
thealpacayarnco.com
Halo

Bijou Basin Ranch
PO Box 154
Elbert, CO 80106
bijoubasinranch.com
Bijou Spun Lhasa Wilderness

Caron
caron.com
Naturally Caron Country, Simply Soft

Drew Emborsky Yarn
drewemborsky.com/yarn
Iconic, Sarcastic

Eucalan
PO Box 374
Paris, Ontario
Canada N3L 3T5
eucalan.com
Wrapture No Rinse Delicate Wash

Fiesta Yarns
fiestayarns.com
Gracie's Lace

Lantern Moon
7911 NE 33rd Dr., Ste. 140
Portland, OR 97211
Destiny circular knitting needles

Lorna's Laces
4229 N. Honore St.
Chicago, IL 60613
lornaslaces.net
Sportmate

**Tahki Stacy Charles/
Filatura Di Crosa**
70-60 83rd St., Bldg. #12
Glendale, NY 11385
tahkistacycharles.com
Nirvana, Superior, Zarina

Tilli Tomas
tillitomas.com
Aspen, Flurries

Trendsetter Yarns
16745 Saticoy St., Ste. 101
Van Nuys, CA 91406
trendsetteryarns.com
Tonalita

INDEX

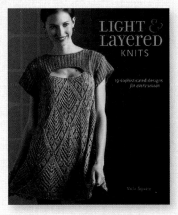